Foreword

Dear reader,

I wrote this book with the same idea in mind as I had for my two vegetarian recipe books: help friends and relatives of vegans to more easily accept the newly chosen lifestyle. Living and eating together may rapidly become a problem, as there may be the impossibility to prepare two separate meals at once (due to time and/or budget), or there may even be a non-acceptance simply due to ignorance. This book won't of course solve all problems at once, but it offers a wide range of savory dishes that surely will satisfy vegans as well as “others”.

However, if the vegan lifestyle has been chosen, there are even more things to consider than for a vegetarian lifestyle. Vegans usually refuse to consume any product that has animal origins. This includes of course meat, but also dairy products as well as eggs, with the simple reasoning that although animals were not killed for the latter two, they had to suffer needlessly nevertheless.

So even when going shopping for food, you'll have to pay attention to detail when it comes to the list of ingredients. Did you know for example that some pasta types are prepared with eggs? Of course there are alternatives like those made with semolina, usually with similar taste. As for dairy products, thankfully there are already a lot of plant-based alternatives like soy, rice or almond milk products.

The key to a savory vegan cuisine lies, in my opinion, in the right use of spices. It is important that, before serving the dish you prepared, you taste it to make sure it isn't bland. When you have checked that and maybe seasoned a bit more if necessary, you'll notice that at least some of the “normals” will start appreciating vegan food as well.

Finally it has to be noted that with the world's population growing at the present rate, some scientists consider veganism as the most viable option in the long run for sustaining our ever-growing numbers with the limited resources our planet has to offer.

In the meantime, I hope you enjoy the dishes provided by this book.

Phil

Contents

Before you start...

- Before you start to cook, I recommend that you first read the whole recipe, make sure you have everything you need, then prepare your ingredients, like washing, coring, peeling, cutting, dicing and so on. Put them into separate bowls, so you have them handy once you have begun heating pots and pans.

- Often enough, you'll find that recipes contain kitchen measures, like
    - Tablespoon (TBSP)
    - Teaspoon (TSP)
    - Cup
    - Pinch
    - And so on

- Cooking is not an exact science, and some light variations in quantity usually don't make a difference (careful with some ingredients like ground clove though). To be successful at it, you need to taste your dish regularly during and after preparation and season it if necessary.

- When working with ingredients that have strong tastes and properties, like chilies, onion, shallot or garlic, it is generally not a bad idea to put on gloves and especially never to rub your eyes during work.

- As for temperature indications, you'll often notice somewhat vague terms like "low", "medium" or "high". Exact measures are difficult to provide due to the large number of available stoves. Here is a small guide to it, if your stove can be regulated between 0 and 9:
    - "low" : 2-4: keeps your dish warm
    - "medium": 5-7: gentle frying and simmering
    - "high": 8-9: boiling

- Ingredients marked with an * are known to cause allergic reactions in some people. Not all potentially dangerous ingredients may be marked. In case of doubt, consult a doctor and your local ministry of health.

- Since this book is translated from the French original, some quantity indications may be a bit unusual, but rest assured, they will lead to savory results.

Aertsoppa

Sweden

Feeds 4

400 g of dried yellow peas
1 TSP of salt
1 onion
1 lemon
4 cloves
*200 g of smoked tofu**
½ TSP of chopped marjoram
½ TSP of chopped thyme
½ TBSP of mustard
1 TSP of salt
1.5 litres of water

Ideally, the preparation of this already begins the day before by pouring the peas into a bowl with enough water to cover them and 1 TSP of salt. That way, they can absorb the water over night and the following preparation will take less time the day after.

Before heating the peas the day after, pour the water off by means of a sieve, then rinse them until the water pouring off is clear. Put them into a large pot with all of the water and 1 TSP of salt. Heat the pot at a medium temperature and let it simmer for about an hour.

In the meantime, you may dice the tofu into pieces as large as half a finger and peel the onion. Take the cloves and stick them into the onion. Once the pot has simmered for an hour, put in the onion and keep it going at medium temperature for another 30 minutes. After this, take out the onion and add the thyme, the marjoram as well as the mustard. Mix, then puree it with a hand blender, and add the tofu dices. Taste and season if necessary, then serve the soup. You may add a slice of lemon and some chopped parsley or marjoram as decoration.

As peas have been cultivated for millennia in Europe, they have been eaten since times immemorial, but mostly by the poorer population. In Scandinavia and especially in Sweden, the pea soup is mostly served on Thursdays as a preparation to fast on Friday. Traditionally, there are pancakes served as a dessert after, as some sort of excuse for this simple yet satiating meal.

Bean Soup

Luxembourg

Feeds 4

400 g of green flat beans
400 g of potatoes
2 TBSP of wheat flour*
1 vegetable stock cube
1 TSP of chopped savory
1 laurel leaf
50 ml of neutral oil (like sunflower)
2 TBSP of vinegar
Salt and pepper
2 litres of water

Rinse the beans and cut off their ends. Dice them into bits as large as a finger.

Put the vegetable stock cube into a large pot along with the water and bring it to a boil. Reduce the heat to medium, add the beans as well as the laurel leaf and let them simmer for about 50 minutes. Meanwhile peel, rinse and dice the potatoes into bits as large as a finger. Heat up the oil in another pot, add the flour and stir until the mix has become golden in color.

Take the pot off the heat and add some vegetable stock from the other pot (without beans) until the mix becomes fluid. Once the 50 minutes from above have passed, pour the mix into the pot with the beans, add the vinegar, the savory as well as the potato dices. Let it simmer for another 15 minutes at medium temperature. Taste one of the potato dices to see if they are soft enough, then add pinches of salt and pepper, taste and season if necessary.

The soup is usually served with a bottle of vinegar and white wine, so everyone can give his portion a personal touch.

The small country in the heart of Europe is not only home to numerous institutions of the European Union, but it also houses a multitude of restaurants with dishes from all over the world. However, this does not mean that the traditional Luxembourgish cuisine has nothing to offer by itself. The Bean Soup or “Bouneschlupp” in the local tongue, has its origins in the agricultural past. While the original version is served along with bacon and a kind of local sausage, it does not lose any of its authenticity by leaving them out.

Bean Soup

Serbia

Feeds 4

300 g of white baked beans
4 carrots
1 leek
2 onions
1 clove of garlic
200 g of peeled tomatoes
300 g of potatoes
*200 g of smoked tofu**
1 yellow bell pepper
4 TBSP of neutral oil (like sunflower)
1 TSP of red paprika powder
½ TSP of salt
½ TSP of ground pepper
1 TSP of chopped marjoram
1 TSP of chopped parsley
2 TBSP of vinegar
600 ml of water

If the beans are dried, it is recommended that you put them in a large bowl with water the night before the preparation. Before beginning to prepare, you should then let them simmer first in a pot of water at low temperature for about an hour.

Meanwhile, peel the carrots, the potatoes, the garlic and the onions. Dice the potatoes as well as the onions into pieces as large as a finger and cut the carrots into half-discs. Chop the garlic. Dice the tofu into pieces half as large as a finger. Rinse the leek and cut it into rings. Wash, core and dice the bell pepper as large as a finger.

Fry the tofu in a pan with 2 TBSP of oil for 4 to 5 minutes at medium temperature to make it a little more firm.

Heat the remaining 2 TBSP of oil in a pot at medium temperature, add the onions as well as the garlic and fry them for 1 to 2 minutes. Pour in the water, the potatoes, the tomatoes, the leek, the carrots, the salt, the pepper, the paprika powder and the marjoram. Let it all simmer for 30 minutes, then add the vinegar, the bell pepper, the beans (without any fluid) as well as the tofu and let it simmer for another 10 minutes.

Taste and season if necessary with vinegar, salt and/or pepper. Serve the dish in soup plates and spread some chopped parsley on top.

Variations of this dish are not only found in Serbia where it is named “Pasulj”, but also in neighboring countries like Croatia where it is called “Grah”.

Beijing Soup

Feeds 4

1 shallot
1 clove of garlic
3 cm of ginger
150 g of bamboo sprouts
200 g of soy sprouts*
100 g of baby corn
1 Chinese cabbage
100 g Shitake mushrooms
3 TBSP of soy sauce*
2 TBSP of tomato puree
3 TBSP of sesame oil*
3 TBSP of rice vinegar (or regular vinegar)
1 TSP of Sambal Oelek paste
2 TBSP of sugar
1 TSP of salt
1 vegetable stock cube
3 TBSP of corn starch
1 litre of water

First chop the garlic and the shallot, then peel and grate the ginger. Rinse the cabbage and the mushrooms, then cut them into thin slices. Cut the baby corn into 3 or 4 pieces. Fry the shallot, the ginger and the garlic in a large pot with 2 TBSP of oil for 1 to 2 minutes at medium temperature. Pour in the water as well as the soy sauce and bring this mixture to a boil. Add the mushrooms, the soy, the bamboo sprouts, the baby corn as well as the tomato puree.

Stir the mixture, then bring it to a boil again and add the vinegar, the sugar and a pinch of salt. Reduce the temperature to a medium level and let it simmer for 2 to 3 minutes. Crumble the stock cube into the pot with the soup and add the cabbage bands as well as the Sambal Oelek paste.

Stir and let it simmer for 5 to 6 minutes at medium temperature. In the end, taste it and season with salt, sugar and/or Sambal Oelek if necessary.

The Beijing Soup is, as its name indicates, a specialty of the Chinese capital, where it is also known under the name of "sweet and sour soup". The regular version with meat stock is quite popular in south-eastern Asia with its ingredients depending on the region.

Bigos

Feeds 4

Poland

*400 g of smoked tofu**
4 large potatoes
1 head of white cabbage
500 g of sauerkraut (pickled cabbage)
400 g of peeled tomatoes
200 g of mushrooms
2 apples of sour taste
3 onions
2 cloves of garlic
2 TSP of chili flakes
1 bay leaf
3 TBSP of tomato puree
3 TBSP of red paprika powder
1 vegetable stock cube
3 TBSP of neutral oil (like sunflower)
1 glass of red wine (ca. 100 ml)
1 TSP of chopped oregano
1 TSP of caraway
Salt and pepper
Chopped parsley
200 ml of water

To begin, rinse the cabbage and slice it into thin bands as long as a thumb. Peel then chop the garlic and dice the onions into pieces as large as a finger. Wash the apples, core them, then dice them into pieces as large as half a finger. Rinse the mushrooms and cut them into thin slices.

Heat the oil in a large pot at medium temperature, then add the garlic as well as the onions and fry them for 1 to 2 minutes before adding the tofu. Keep going for another 1 to 2 minutes, then put in the tomatoes, the cabbage, the sauerkraut (without fluid), the mushrooms as well as the bay leaf and let it simmer for 4 to 5 minutes. Then add the chili flakes, the paprika powder, the caraway, the oregano as well as pinches of salt and pepper.

Dissolve the stock cube in a bowl with the water, then add the tomato puree and the wine. Pour it all into the pot, cover it and let it simmer for an hour while stirring regularly.

In the meantime, you can peel the potatoes and put them in another pot along with salted water. Bring it to a boil until the potatoes have become soft. When the vegetable mixture is ready, put it on the plates first, then a potato on top with some chopped parsley as decoration.

Variations: Instead of the entire potatoes, the dish can also be served with potato puree or simply with slices of bread. You can also add a few juniper berries (6 or 7 depending on your taste), some carrots or dried plums.

The name of this dish simply translates to « sauerkraut » in Polish. It has to be noted that it used to be quite popular in Poland after World War II and it was subsidized (among others) by the government so that it was affordable for the entire population.

Bread Soup

Feeds 4

Germany

250 g hardenend bread
2 vegetable stock cubes
2 onions
1 clove of garlic
6 TBSP of neutral oil (like sunflower)
½ TSP of caraway powder
2 TSP of freshly chopped chive
½ TSP of salt
½ of ground pepper
½ TSP of chopped oregano
1 litre of water

To begin with, peel the garlic and the onions, then chop them. Cut the bread into pieces as large as a finger.

Pour 2 TBSP of oil into a pan and roast the bread pieces in it at medium temperature for about 6 to 8 minutes while turning them often. When they have become golden, put them aside in a bowl.

Take the same pan, put the remaining oil into it at low temperature and fry the onions and the garlic in it along with the caraway powder for 5 to 6 minutes. Put them aside in a bowl as well.

Pour the water into a large pot, bring it to the boil and dissolve the stock cubes in it. Add the oregano, the salt and the pepper. Taste and season with some more salt and/or pepper if necessary.

To serve the Bread Soup, divide the bread as well as the onion-garlic mix onto soup plates, pour the stock over it and spread some chopped chive on top for decoration.

Variation: As in some regions of Germany the soup is also served with bacon in it, you may substitute that for 200 g of smoked tofu* which you dice into pieces as large as half a finger and which you then add to the pan with the onions and the garlic to fry them.

Although fairly common in all of Europe, this sort of soup was mainly eaten in Germany after World War II, when meat and dairy products were scarce and expensive. Today, it is a welcome opportunity to use old bread and transform it into a meal.

Brunswick Stew

Feeds 4

400 g of potatoes
*400 g of smoked tofu**
300 g of sweetcorn
400 g of peeled tomatoes
300 g of green Lima beans
2 onions
5 TBSP of neutral oil
1 TSP of ground pepper
2 TSP of salt
2 TSP of sugar
Salt and pepper
1 litre of water

Peel the potatoes and cut them into mouthfuls while you dice the tofu into pieces as large as a finger. Peel the onions and cut them in the same way. Drain the corn and the beans of their fluid.

Heat 2 TBSP of oil in a pan at medium temperature, then fry the tofu dices in it for 4 to 5 minutes. Reduce the heat to a very low level after.

Take a large pot, put the potato pieces in, cover them with water and add the salt. Bring the pot to the boil, then reduce the temperature to a medium level, add the pepper as well as the sugar and let it simmer until the potatoes have become soft.

Put in the tomatoes as well as the beans and let them simmer for 15 minutes. Reduce the temperature to a low level, add the corn and the remaining oil, let them simmer for another 40 minutes, then add the tofu and keep going for 10 more minutes.

The stew should be a little thick, if it is not the case, add some potato starch.

There are two contestants claiming the right to have invented this dish from the Southern U.S.. On one side, there is the city of Brunswick in the state of Georgia, on the other there is the county of Brunswick in the state of Virginia.

Bruschetta

Italy

Feeds 4

5 tomatoes
1 onion
2 cloves of garlic
2 Ciabatta breads (500 g each) or 1 Baguette
2 TBSP of chopped basil
*50 g of vegan Parmesan-type cheese**
200 ml of olive oil
Salt and pepper

Wash the tomatoes, core them and dice them into pieces as large as half a finger. Peel the onion, then dice it the same size as the tomatoes. Peel the garlic, then chop it. Put it into a bowl along with the the olive oil as well as pinches of salt and pepper. Stir, then leave it alone for 10 minutes. Grate the cheese in the meantime.

Preheat your oven at 180°C, then cut the bread into slices as thick as a thumb. Mix the tomatoes, the onions, the cheese and the basil in another large bowl. Put the bread slices on an oven tray with a baking parchment, distribute the oil mixture evenly on them and put them into the oven for about 8 to 10 minutes.

When you have taken them out again, leave the bread slices on the hot tray while you distribute the tomato/onion mix on them. When you are done, put them onto plates and serve them.

The bruschetta can be eaten as a light main course by 3 or 4 people, or the same quantity may be served as antipasti (starters) or appetizers for about 10 people.

Variation: While the described recipe is quite popular in Tuscany, there are other versions like the one from Calabria, where you can replace the tomatoes by red bell peppers and the basil by oregano.

As one might imagine, the bruschetta was a typical meal for poor people for a long time and mostly eaten in the South of Italy. In recent times however, it has established itself as antipasto and numerous Italian restaurants serve it as such.

Cabbage Rolls

Feeds 4

Romania

2 cups of plain rice
1 head of white cabbage
2 onions
1 clove of garlic
2 carrots
1 yellow bell pepper
400 g of tomato puree
50 g of soy granulate*
4 TBSP of neutral oil (like sunflower)
1 vegetable stock cube
2 TBSP of wheat flour*
2 TBSP of sugar
10 TBSP of liquid plant-based cream
½ TSP of chopped dill
Powdered caraway
Chopped basil
Salt and pepper
6 cups of water

Cook the rice by putting it into a pot with the 5 cups of water and a pinch of salt and bringing it to the boil until it has absorbed all the water. Rinse the cabbage, take off its external leaves, put it into a pot, cover it with water, add a pinch of salt, cover the pot and bring it to the boil until its leaves have become soft.

Wash the bell pepper, core it, then dice it as large as half a finger. Peel the carrots as well as the onions and dice them into pieces as large as half a finger as well. Peel and chop the garlic. Heat 2 TBSP of oil in a large pot at medium temperature and fry half of the onions as well as the garlic at medium temperature for 2 to 3 minutes. Add the vegetable dices and keep frying for 4 to 5 minutes while stirring regularly. Pour in half of the boiled rice and mix. Season with pinches of salt, ground pepper, basil as well as caraway and taste. Let this mixture cool off and preheat your oven at 180 °C.

In the meantime, you may prepare the tomato sauce. Heat 2 TBSP of oil in a pot and fry the remaining half of the onions in it at medium temperature for 1 to 2 minutes. Add the last cup of water, the tomato puree, the crushed vegetable stock cube, the sugar and the dill. Stir, bring the pot to the boil, then turn off the heat and taste. Season if necessary.

When the rice and vegetable mix has cooled off, add the soy granulate and the flour. Take the cabbage out of its pot, let all excess water pour off, then take off its leaves. Put one at a time on your work surface, set some rice-vegetable mix on it (depending on its size), roll it and fix it with a wooden toothpick or some special thread for cooking.

Take a glass tray for the oven, put a thin layer of tomato sauce at its bottom, then a layer of rolls, another thin layer of sauce, another layer of rolls and so on until you run out of rolls or sauce. In the end, make sure every roll is covered in sauce and spread the cream on top. Cover the tray with a aluminum foil, then insert it into the oven for 1 hour at 180 °C.

Once the rolls are done, distribute them on your plates with a little sauce and the remaining rice.

This method of preparing a stuffing rolled in plant leaves can be traced back to the Byzantine Empire. Aside from the cabbage leaves, other variants exist, like vine leaves, which the Greek then call “Dolmades”.

California Rolls

Feeds 4

500 g of sushi rice
1 avocado
1 mango
1 banana
1 pack of sesame grains*
*100 g of vegan cream cheese**
10 Nori sheets
50 ml of rice vinegar
1 TBSP of sugar
Wasabi paste
*Soy sauce**
Pickled ginger
950 ml of water

As the California Rolls are by their nature similar to hoso-maki rolls, their preparation is similar as well.

First rinse the rice in a sieve until the water pouring off is clear. Pour it into a large pot along with 900 ml of water and bring it to the boil. Reduce the temperature to a low level and let it soak for about 10 minutes while stirring regularly to avoid the rice sticking to the bottom. Put it into a large bowl afterwards to cool off. Mix the remaining water, the sugar and the vinegar in a smaller bowl, then spread it over the rice.

Peel the avocado, cut it in two, core it, then cut it into thin bands. Repeat the process for the mango and the banana.

Take an appropriate bamboo mat and cover it first with cellophane then put a Nori sheet on it. Cover the entire surface of the Nori in rice as thick as half a finger or less. Carefully slide the Nori off the mat, put cellophane on the rice, turn it upside down so that the cellophane on the rice is at the bottom. Remove the upper cellophane, cover the top side (on the Nori) near one edge with the ingredients of your choice. While keeping them in place with a few fingers, roll the Nori toward the free edge. Be careful no to include any cellophane. Once you are done rolling, cover the whole outer surface of the roll in sesame grains.

Repeat this process until you are either out of rice, Nori sheets or ingredients. The California Rolls are normally served with some wasabi paste, pickled ginger and some soy sauce.

Variation: You can of course use other ingredients as well, like a cucumber or a carrot cut into thin bands.

The California Rolls were, as their name suggests, probably invented by a Japanese chef living in Los Angeles. Their category is called “Ura-maki” in Japanese and is however not a part of the traditional Japanese sushi palette.

Chacalaca

South Africa

Feeds 4

2 cups of plain rice
1 red bell pepper
1 yellow bell pepper
2 carrots
2 onions
100 g of coconut oil
350 g of white baked beans (with fluid)
2 TSP of curry powder
2 TSP of chili flakes
1 vegetable stock cube
Salt and pepper
5 cups of water

First, rinse and core the bell peppers, peel the carrots as well as the onions and dice all of them into bits as large as a finger.

Then pour the oil into a large pot so that it covers the entire bottom and heat it up. When this is the case, raise the temperature to a high level and put in the vegetable stock cube, dissolve it while stirring. Add the diced vegetables and the onions, reduce the temperature to a medium level and let them fry for 20 minutes while stirring constantly. Taste if the carrots are soft enough.

If you want to prepare some rice to go with it, you can do this in the mean time by pouring it along with the water as well as a pinch of salt into a pot. Bring it to a boil and take it off the heat once almost all of the water has been absorbed.

After these 20 minutes, add the baked beans with their fluid, as well as the curry powder and the chili flakes to the first pot. After mixing this, reduce the temperature a little, then let it simmer for another 10 minutes while stirring regularly.

Taste your dish afterwards and if necessary, season it with some salt and/or pepper.

Variation: Another way to prepare the Chacalaca is to replace the yellow bell pepper by a small white cabbage and to add 1 inch of grated ginger.

Usually served with some fish, this ingredient has been replaced by baked beans. As for many other dishes, its composition slightly variates depending on which region the recipe is originating from.

Chili sin Carne

Feeds 4

2 shallots
1 clove of garlic
300 – 400 g of peeled tomatoes
2 red chilies (or more)
200 g of sweetcorn
300 – 400 g of red baked beans
*200 g of smoked tofu**
1 vegetable stock cube
1 TBSP of sugar
4 TBSP of neutral oil (like sunflower)
1 TSP of ground pepper
Salt and pepper
Hot Sauce
100 ml of water

First of all, rinse and core the chilies, then slice them. Dice the tofu into bits as large as a finger and chop the garlic as well as the shallots.

Mix 2 TBSP of oil with the ground pepper in a bowl, pour the tofu dices in and make sure every side is covered with oil. After that, put the remaining 2 TBSP of oil into a large pot, along with the shallots, the chilies and the garlic. Fry them for 1 to 2 minutes at medium temperature. Dissolve the vegetable stock cube in the water and add it along with the peeled tomatoes to the pot.

Let the mixture cook for 5 minutes at medium temperature while stirring regularly, then add the sweetcorn as well as the red baked beans and let them simmer for another 10 minutes.

Meanwhile, pour the bowl with tofu and oil into a pan and fry it at medium temperature until it has a golden color. When this is the case, pour it into the pot, add the sugar as well as a pinch of salt and pepper and stir.

Season to taste with salt, pepper and/or some hot sauce.

Originating from the texmex cuisine and especially from Texas, the Chili con carne is often erroneously attributed to the Mexican cuisine, while it certainly has some of its properties. Its vegetarian counterpart, the chili sin carne does not lose its remarkable taste by replacing the meat with smoked tofu.

Chop Suey

Feeds 4

*200 g smoked tofu**
300 g of bamboo sprouts
200 g of soy sprouts*
200 g of mushrooms
4 carrots
2 cups of basmati rice
1 clove of garlic
3 cm of ginger
4 TBSP of sesame oil*
2 TSP of sugar
3 TBSP of potato starch
Sambal Oelek
150 ml of soy sauce*
150 ml of water
5 cups of water

About 1 hour before beginning with the main preparations, you may mix the marinade. For this, pour the 150 ml of water, the soy sauce, the sugar and the starch into a bowl and mix them. Dice the tofu into pieces as large as a finger, put it into the marinade and leave it be for 40 minutes.

Wash the mushrooms, then cut them into slices as thick as half a finger or less. Peel the garlic and the ginger, chop the first and grate the latter. Pour the fluid off of the soy and bamboo sprouts. Peel the carrots and cut them into thin discs.

Wash the rice in a sieve, then pour it into a small pot with 5 cups of water and a pinch of salt. Heat it at high temperature until it has absorbed all water. Stir regularly to prevent it from sticking to the bottom.

Heat the oil in a large pan or a wok at medium temperature, add the tofu without its marinade, the carrots, the garlic as well as the ginger and fry them until the carrots are soft enough for you. They should however remain a little crunchy. Put in the soy and bamboo sprouts as well as the mushrooms and keep frying at medium temperature for about 4 to 5 minutes. Pour in the marinade and bring it to the boil until the sauce begins to thicken.

Taste, season with salt, pepper and/or Sambal Oelek and serve the Chop Suey along with the rice.

Variations: Translated from Cantonese, “Chop Suey” approximately means “various leftovers”, so it can be prepared with numerous other vegetable leftovers you still have got in your fridge, like broccoli, bell peppers, spring onions, onions or leek.

When it comes to the origins of this dish, there are two theories. The first sees a Chinese chef who immigrated to the United States as its inventor, while the second sees the origins in the Southern Taishan region in China.

Couscous

Feeds 4

Northern Africa

200 g of semolina
1 red bell pepper
1 shallot
60 g of dried raisins
2 TBSP of olive oil
1 vegetable stock cube
1 pinch of salt
½ TSP of parsley
1 pinch of cumin
1 pinch of coriander
1 dosen mint leaves
500 ml of water

Rinse, core and dice the bell pepper into bits as large as a finger. Dissolve the stock cube in the water and chop the shallot. Put the shallot into a pan along with the oil and fry it for 1 to 2 minutes at medium temperature, then pour in the stock afterwards.

Add the semolina, the dried raisins as well as the spices and let them simmer at low temperature for about 10 minutes, so that the semolina may suck up the water.

In the end, add the bell pepper dices, stir, taste it and if necessary, season with some more spices and serve the dish still warm, with 3 or 4 mint leaves as decoration.

The couscous, undoubtedly one of the best-known representatives of the Arabian cuisine, is traditionally prepared in a special pot in which the semolina is placed in a container above the stock with the vegetables, so that it may absorb the vapors of it. To personalize the dish, it may also be served with the “Ras el-Hanout” spice mixture and the “Harissa” hot sauce.

Curry vegetables

Feeds 4

Jamaica

500 g of sweet potatoes
2 mangos
2 plantain bananas
3 carrots
4 lemons
1 clove of garlic
3 cm of ginger
1 onion
1 cup of basmati rice
250 g of baked red beans in fluid
800 ml of coconut milk
4 TBSP of coconut butter
4 TSP of curry powder
5 TBSP of wheat flour*
2 TSP of chili flakes
1 TSP of chopped thyme
1 TSP of Garam Masala spices
2 TBSP of cane sugar
Salt and pepper
Water

Peel then chop the garlic. Press the lemons to obtain their juice. Peel the sweet potatoes as well as the mangoes and cut them into sticks as large as a finger and as long as a thumb. Peel the carrots, the onion and the ginger, cut the carrots into thin slices, chop the onion and grate the ginger.

Heat about half of the coconut butter in a pot at medium temperature, then add the rice. Stir well during 1 to 2 minutes, so that each grain of rice is covered in butter. Pour in about half of the coconut milk, the thyme, the red beans (without fluid), half of the garlic as well as pinches of salt and pepper. Pour in some water until it barely covers the contents of the pot. Bring it to the boil, then reduce the temperature to a medium level and let it simmer until the rice has absorbed all fluid.

Put the lemon juice into a bowl and mix it with the sugar, then peel the bananas and cut them in two along their axis. Marinate them in the lemon juice for 8 to 10 minutes. Spread 1 TSP of chili flakes on them, then turn them in the flour, in a way that they are completely covered. Heat the remaining coconut butter in a large pan at medium temperature, the fry the bananas in it until they have become golden.

Heat another pot at medium temperature, put in the sweet potato sticks as well as 1 TSP of chili flakes and the curry. Stir for a few moments, then add the remaining coconut milk, 1 TBSP of lemon juice with sugar, the mango, the carrots, the ginger as well as the onion. Mix, then let it simmer for 10 minutes.

Add the Garam Masala and let it simmer for another 15 minutes. Taste and season if necessary. The sauce should be a little thick, if it is not, add some starch. Serve the fried bananas, the rice and the curry vegetables on a plate.

The Jamaican cuisine, as well as the Caribbean cuisine in general, is marked by European, Asian and African influences. Most dishes are intense and spicy in taste, perhaps a reflection of the healthy local life attitude.

Fajitas

Feeds 4

Mexico

*200 g of smoked tofu**
3 bell peppers: red, yellow, green
1 shallot
1 clove of garlic
4 TBSP of neutral oil (sunflower)
300 g of baked red beans (with fluid)
8 or more wheat tortillas*
*300 g – 400 g of plant-based yoghurt**
*200 g of grated vegan cheese**
200 g of iceberg salad
Salt and pepper
Vegan Guacamole sauce*

First of all, preheat the oven at 80°C, rinse the vegetables and core them if necessary, then chop the shallot and the garlic. Cut the bell pepper into thin strips large as half a finger and long as a thumb. Wash the beans and put them aside in a bowl to be heated in the oven afterwards.

Cut the salad into thin slices as long as a thumb and put it into a second bowl. Put the grated vegan cheese into a third bowl.

Heat up 2 TBSP of oil along with the shallot as well as the garlic in a pan and fry them for 1 to 2 minutes at medium temperature. Add the bell pepper and let them fry at the same temperature for 8 to 10 minutes. After this, put them into a fourth bowl. Dice the tofu, put it into the pan with 2 TBSP of oil and fry it for 3 to 4 minutes at medium temperature. Season to taste with some salt and/or pepper if necessary. Put it into a fifth bowl when you are done.

Finally put a plate with the tortillas, as well as the bowls with the beans, the bell peppers and the tofu into the oven for 5 minutes before serving. Careful though when taking them out again, the plate and bowls will be hot. Pour the Salsa sauce into another bowl and serve it along with the rest of the dish. If you want to prepare the sauce yourself, consider preparing it before the fajitas.

Variation: You may of course leave one or two bell peppers aside to replace them with a small glass of sweetcorn, which you rinse before serving and/or 2 tomatoes that are rinsed, cored and cut into thin slices as large as half a finger and as long as a thumb.

Even today the origins of this dish are not very clear. Some believe them to be Mexican or central American, while others think it developed in the texmex cuisine as it used to be a typical cowboy meal.

Feijoada

Feeds 4

Brazil

400 g of dried black beans (600 g if not dried)
*400 g of smoked tofu**
2 onions
1 clove of garlic
1 shallot
2 TBSP of olive oil
2 bay leaves
3 cubes of vegetable stock
3 oranges
2 TBSP of curry powder
1 TBSP of red paprika powder
1 TBSP of black peppercorns
Salt and ground pepper
2 cups of plain rice
Starch if necessary
5 cups of water
Water

If your beans are dried, it is recommended that you put them in a bowl with water the night before the preparation, so they have time to absorb some of it. Once you are ready for the rest of the preparation, peel the onions as well as the garlic, then chop them. Dice the tofu into pieces as large as a finger.

Put the beans first into a sieve to get rid of the excess water, then into a large pot with enough fresh water to cover them as thick as a finger's width and bring them to the boil. Add the bay leaves as well as 2 stock cubes. Put in the onions, the garlic, the curry, the paprika powder as well as the peppercorns and a pinch of salt. Let this mixture simmer for one hour at high temperature.

When about 40 minutes have passed, peel the shallot, chop it and put it in a pot with the oil and fry it for 1 to 2 minutes at medium temperature. Add the rice and let it fry with the shallot as well as the oil for 1 minute, then add the cups of water along with the last vegetable stock cube. Stir, then bring the mixture to the boil until the rice has absorbed all water. Pay attention however that it does not stick to the bottom.

Rinse then press two oranges to obtain their juice. Cut the third into slices for decoration.

When the hour is up for the large pot, add the tofu dices as well as the orange juice and take out the bay leaves. Reduce the temperature to a medium level and let it simmer for 10 minutes. Taste and season if necessary with salt and/or pepper. If the sauce is too fluid, add some starch.

Serve the feijoada with the rice and a few slices of orange on top as decoration.

Although originating from Portugal, this stew not only contains beans in its original form, but high quantities of meat as well (which were replaced by a little tofu), and it is mostly eaten in Brazil. There are however variations to be found in other former colonies of Portugal, like Angola, Mozambique and Macao.

Focaccia

Italy

Feeds 4

450 g of wheat flour*
125 g of potatoes
1 pack of yeast (~40 g)
1 TSP of salt
12 cherry tomatoes
1 clove of garlic
80 – 100 g of olives
1 TSP of oregano
6 TBSP of olive oil
180 ml of water

First of all, peel the potatoes and let them boil in salted water until they have become soft, let them cool off and finally mash them to a puree. Put the (hand warm) water into a bowl, dissolve the yeast in it and add a pinch of flour, cover the bowl and leave it alone for a few minutes.

Meanwhile, cut the cherry tomatoes in two. Then pour the flour into the bowl with the water and the yeast, along with the potato puree, the garlic, the salt and the oregano. Knead this dough for about 10 minutes, then put it back into the bowl, cover it and put it in a warm place to let it rise during 2 to 3 hours.

Half an hour before continuing, preheat the oven at 220 °C. Cover an oven tray with baking parchment, divide the dough into 4 portions of the same size and place 2 or 4 of them (depending on the tray's size) on it. Flatten the dough until it is as thick as a finger. Now put the olives and the cherry tomato halves on it and push them gently halfway in. Cover the Focaccias in olive oil, preferably using a brush and put the plate into the oven for about 20 minutes while regularly checking that the Focaccias do not get too dark. After 10 minutes, open the oven for a short while to crush the cherry tomatoes with a spoon.

After taking them out 10 minutes later, do not worry if the tomatoes' skins have darkened, you can just take them off before serving.

Variations: As with numerous other dishes, the Focaccia too comes in different forms and compositions depending which region the recipe originates from; this one is from the Apulia region in the South-East of Italy.

In Tuscany, it is prepared with anchovies and red onions, if you replace the anchovies with 100 g of smoked and salted tofu*, you will obtain a vegan alternative to it.

In Lombardy to the north, the dough is not prepared with salt, but with sugar.

The focaccia is not, as one might imagine, served as a side dish, but rather as breakfast or a light meal during the day.

Fried noodles with vegetables

Feeds 3

China

8 TBSP of sesame oil*
1 red bell pepper
1 onion
2 red chilies
2 carrots
1 TBSP of fried onions
10 TBSP of tomato puree
8 TBSP of soy sauce*
1 TBSP of sugar
2 TSP of hot curry powder
4 TSP of red paprika powder
250 g of asian noodles

Begin by bringing the water to a boil with a pinch of salt to cook the noodles as indicated on their packaging. Once they are done, drain their water and put them aside in a bowl.

Meanwhile, you can prepare the vegetables: chop the onion, core and cut the bell pepper into thin slices as long as half a thumb. Peel the carrots and cut them in the same way. Core the chilies, then cut them into thin slices.

Prepare the sauce in a bowl by pouring in the tomato puree, the soy sauce, the sugar, the curry as well as the red paprika powder and mix it thoroughly.

Heat up a wok or a large pan with 4 TBSP of oil, the onions as well as the chilies and fry them for 1 to 2 minutes at medium temperature. After this, add the bell pepper, the carrots and the sauce to let them simmer for 10 minutes while stirring regularly.

Meanwhile take another pan, pour in 4 TBSP of oil, heat it up to medium temperature, put the noodles in and fry them for 5 to 6 minutes while turning them often.

Finally add the noodles and the fried onions to the wok, mix them well and let them simmer for 1 to 2 minutes at medium temperature, then taste and if necessary season some more.

A specialty of Asian restaurants everywhere, fried noodles with beef, pork, chicken or seafood are quite popular. Their vegetarian alternative, fried noodles with vegetables, are maybe a little less known. However by preparing them yourself, you have both the advantages of knowing your ingredients' origins and a more authentic taste unaltered by flavor enhancers.

Gazpacho andaluz

Spain

Feeds 4

600 g of tomatoes
1 green bell pepper
1 cucumber
2 cloves of garlic
300 g of white bread
4 TBSP of olive oil
2 TBSP of vinegar
2 vegetable stock cubes
½ TSP of salt
½ TSP of ground pepper
500 ml of water

Wash the vegetables, take off the green bit of the tomatoes, cut them into mouthfuls and core them. Peel the cucumber, cut it into small dices and keep about one fourth of them as decoration for later. Core the bell pepper and dice it as large as half a finger and keep one fourth of it for later. Take off the bread's crust and put its white parts into the same bowl as the vegetables.

Peel the garlic and chop it. Put the stock cubes as well as the salt into the water and stir until they have been dissolved. Pour the water and the garlic into the bowl with the vegetables and the bread, then puree them with a hand blender.

Once you are done with this, add the oil and the vinegar, mix, taste and season some more with vinegar, salt and/or pepper. Put the gazpacho into the fridge for about half an hour.

Take the cucumber as well as the bell pepper pieces you had put aside before and dice them into pieces as large as half a finger. When the gazpacho has been in the fridge, pour it into soup plates, add the vegetable cubes as decoration and serve it cold.

Since it is a cold soup by tradition, the gazpacho is best eaten on hot summer days.

Variations: Depending on the region on the Iberian peninsula, almonds and fresh grapes are added as well. For more frostier days, the gazpacho can be heated as well and you may add 200 g of potatoes.

If you prefer your gazpacho to be more red in color, use a red instead of a green bell pepper.

The origins of the gazpacho are to be found in times where the Iberian peninsula was occupied by Arab troops, and at that time, tomatoes and bell peppers were not yet part of it, since the were only later imported from the New World to Europe after Christoph Columbus discovered the American continent (again). It was only in the 18th century that they became part of the gazpacho.

Goulash

Feeds 4

Hungary

150 g of soy flakes*
*200 g of smoked tofu**
1 cube of vegetable stock
5 TBSP of neutral oil (like sunflower)
4 TBSP of tomato puree
2 cloves of garlic
1 large onion
1 red bell pepper
1 green bell pepper
1 carrot
2 TBSP of red paprika powder
1 chili
Salt and pepper
½ glass of red wine
1 to 2 TBSP of potato starch if needed
1 litre of water

First pour the soy flakes into a pot filled with the water as well as the vegetable stock and bring it to a boil. Reduce its temperature to a minimum, then let the flakes absorb the liquid for 10 minutes before pouring the rest into another bowl and setting the flakes aside for later.

Meanwhile chop the onion and the garlic, core the bell pepper and the chili, dice them into bits as large as a finger or cut them into thin slices respectively. Peel the carrot and slice it as well. Dice the tofu into pieces as large as a finger.

Heat up 2 TBSP in a large pan at medium temperature with the shallot, the garlic, the chili as well as the tofu dices and fry them until they get a slightly golden color.

Heat the rest of the oil in a large pot, along with the soy flakes as well as the vegetables and let them fry for 3 to 4 minutes at medium temperature. Add the tomato puree, the wine, the remaining vegetable stock, the paprika powder as well as pinches of salt and pepper. Put in the pan's contents as well, stir it and let it simmer at medium temperature for about half an hour while stirring regularly.

In the end, taste your dish and season it with some more salt and pepper if needed. The liquid should be a little thick, if it is not, add 1 or 2 TBSP of potato starch at your liking.

The origins of the Goulash are found in medieval times, when it did not yet contain bell peppers, but when it was a simple shepherd's soup based on roasted meat and onions.

Harira

Morocco

Feeds 4

2 onions
1 cup of dried greens lentils
1 cup of chickpeas
400 g of peeled tomatoes
1 stem of branch celery
2 cloves of garlic
1 lemon
100 g of wheat flour*
3 TBSP of neutral oil
1 vegetable stock cube
100 g of small pasta
3 cm of ginger
½ TSP of Harissa sauce
1 TSP of turmeric
½ TSP of cinnamon powder
½ TSP of ground caraway
1 TBSP of chopped parsley
Salt and pepper
1.2 litres of water

A few hours or even the night before the preparation, it is recommended that you put the lentils into one bowl of water and the chickpeas into another so they can soak. One hour before the preparation, pour off the water, put the chickpeas into a pot, cover them with fresh water in a way that the water is about a thumb's width above the lentils. Bring it to the boil until they have softened, then pour the water off.

In the meantime, you may peel the onions and dice them into pieces as large as a finger. Wash the celery, cut off its leaves for later and cut it into half-rings as thick as half a finger. Peel then chop the garlic and grate the ginger. Dissolve the stock cube in the water. Heat the oil in a large pot at medium temperature, add the celery, the garlic and the onions and let them fry for 2 to 3 minutes. Put in the ginger, the Harissa sauce, the turmeric, the cinnamon, the caraway, the parsley as well as pinches of salt and pepper. Let it fry for 1 to 2 more minutes while stirring constantly.

Pour the vegetable stock in, along with the tomatoes, the chickpeas and the lentils. Bring it to the boil, then reduce the temperature to a medium level and let it simmer for 30 minutes while stirring regularly. Add the pasta, taste and season if necessary with salt, pepper and/or Harissa sauce.

Let the pot simmer for another 5 to 6 minutes. Rinse then cut the lemon into slices, then cut those into quarters. Check if the pasta is soft enough, then serve the soup. As for decoration, add a few lemon quarter plus some chopped parsley or celery leaves.

This soup is typically eaten in Morocco and other Arabian countries during the Ramadan, the Muslim fasting month. It is of course only eaten after sunset in that case. Versions with some added meat are to be found, but also with hard-boiled eggs.

Imam bayildi

Feeds 4

Turkey

4 large aubergines
300 g of peeled and chopped tomatoes
5 TBSP of neutral oil
3 cloves of garlic
4 onions
½ TSP of salt
½ TSP of ground pepper
1 TSP of sugar
1 TSP of chopped parsley

Wash the aubergines and scratch off their skin on 2 opposite sides. Cut them in two along their axis and scoop them out. Heat up 3 TBSP of oil in a large pan at medium temperature and fry the aubergines in it on both sides until they are golden in color. Let them cool off while you prepare the sauce.

Peel the onions and the garlic, cut then onions into thin slices while you chop the garlic. Keep a dozen onions rings as decoration for later. Heat 2 TBSP of oil in a large pan and fry the onions and the garlic in it for 2 to 3 minutes, then add the tomatoes. Let this mixture simmer until there is no more fluid. Then add the salt, the pepper as well as the sugar. Taste and season some more if necessary.

Place the aubergines in a large pan, spread some salt as well as pepper onto them, then pour the sauce on them. Now pour some salted water into the pan until it is about half a finger high.

Let the pan simmer at medium temperature for 20 minutes. Take the aubergines out of the pan, put some remaining onion rings on top and serve it on plates.

Translated from Turkish, the name of this dish means approximately "the imam was shaken", which is not surprising considering the quantity of garlic involved.

Irish Stew

Feeds 4

Ireland

*200 g of smoked tofu**
300 g of potatoes
300 g of carrots
1 kohlrabi
1 leek
1 parsnip
1 shallot
1 clove of garlic
1 TBSP of chopped parsley
½ TSP of caraway
½ TSP of chopped thyme
½ TSP of nutmeg powder
3 TBSP of neutral oil (like sunflower)
1 vegetable stock cube
½ TSP of salt
½ TSP of ground pepper
1 – 2 TBSP of starch if needed
Salt and pepper
900 ml of water

Begin by washing the vegetables, peel them if needed and dice the potatoes, the kohlrabi, the parsnip and the tofu into pieces as large as a finger. Slice the carrots and the leek into discs as large as half a finger. Peel then chop the shallot and the garlic.

Dissolve the stock cube in the water and heat the oil in a large pot. Add the shallot, the garlic and the tofu and fry them for 2 to 3 minutes at medium temperature. Remove the tofu and put it in a bowl for later. Put in the remaining vegetables (without the potatoes) and let them simmer for another 4 to 5 minutes while stirring regularly.

Pour in the water with the stock, the parsley, the thyme, the caraway, the nutmeg, the pepper and the salt. Stir, heat it up for a few minutes and taste. Season if necessary, then cover the pot, reduce the temperature to a low level and let it simmer for 50 minutes.

Put in the potato dices as well as the tofu and let the pot simmer at a low temperature for another 15 minutes. Taste again and check if the potatoes are soft enough.

Variation: Fulde Stew: Replace the parsnip by ½ a head of white cabbage.

As for many stews around the world, the Irish Stew ("Stobhach Gaelach" in Gaelic) has its origins the past centuries as a dish of poorer people. Although the traditional lamb meat has been replaced with tofu here, this Irish stew remains quite copious and satiating.

Jambalaya

United States of America

Feeds 4

1 sheaf of celery
1 onion
2 carrots
1 green bell pepper
1 clove of garlic
*200 g of smoked tofu**
400 g of peeled tomatoes
2 cups of plain rice
2 TBSP of neutral oil (like sunflower)
*½ TSP of powdered nutmeg**
1 TSP of ground pepper
½ TSP of salt
3 TSP of red paprika powder
1 TSP of chopped oregano
2 TSP of chopped thyme
½ TSP of cumin powder
½ TSP of chili flakes
1 vegetable stock cube
Salt and pepper
375 ml of water

To begin with, peel the carrots, the onion and the garlic. Cut the carrots into small sticks as large as half a finger and as long as a thumb. Chop the onion and the garlic. Rinse the celery, take off its leaves, then cut it into half-rings as large as a finger. Dice the tofu into pieces as large as half a finger. Wash the bell pepper, core it and dice it into pieces as large as a finger. Dissolve the stock cube in the water in a bowl.

Heat the oil in a large pot at medium temperature, put in the carrots, the bell pepper, the celery, the garlic as well as the onion and fry them for 2 to 3 minutes. Add the rice and roast it for a few moments, then pour in the water with the stock cube, the tomatoes, the nutmeg powder, the pepper, the salt, the paprika powder, the oregano, the thyme, the chili flakes as well as the cumin powder, then stir this mixture.

Cover the pot, reduce the temperature to a low level and let it simmer until the rice has absorbed most of the water. When it is "al dente", add the tofu and let it simmer some more until the rice is soft enough. Taste and season some more with the spices if necessary.

Variation: If you prefer quinoa to rice, you may use the same quantity instead of the rice.

The Jambalaya is part of the Cajun cuisine of the Southern United States, whose main ingredients are onions, green bell peppers and celery. Its origins are probably in the Spanish paella, since the Spanish were to be found in many places in the New World after its discovery.

Japchae

Feeds 4

Korea

300 g of vermicelli noodles
2 carrots
200 g of mushrooms (like Shitake)
200 g of spinach
1 spring onion
3 TBSP of rice vinegar
6 TBSP of sesame oil*
5 TBSP of soy sauce*
1 TSP of sesame grains*
½ TSP of sugar
Salt

Cook the vermicelli according the instructions on their package, cut them into strings as long as a thumb and let them cool off. Rinse the spinach as well as the mushrooms and peel the carrots. Cut all of them into thin bands.

Wash the spring onion, then slice it into thin rings. Heat 2 TBSP of oil in a large pan and fry the spring onion, the mushrooms, the carrots and the spinach for 3 to 4 minutes at medium temperature. After this, mix them with the vermicelli.

Prepare the dressing for the salad by mixing the soy sauce, the remaining 1 TBSP of sesame oil, the vinegar, the sugar and a pinch of salt in a bowl. Taste and season some more if necessary, then pour it over the salad and let it cool further for half an hour.

Serve the salad on plates or in bowls and spread some sesame grains on top as for decoration.

The Japchae normally accompanies meat dishes, and yet another interesting fact is that Korean vermicelli noodles are made from the starch of sweet potatoes.

Kisir

Feeds 4

Turkey

2 cups of bulgur
1 lemon
1 cucumber
3 tomatoes
3 spring onions
4 TBSP of neutral oil (like sunflower)
3 TSP of red paprika powder
3 TBSP of tomato puree
½ TSP of cumin powder
1 TBSP of chopped parsley
Salt
2 ½ cups of water

To begin with, press the lemon to obtain its juice. Heat 2 TBSP of oil in a large pot, add the tomato puree and the red paprika powder and let this simmer for 1 to 2 minutes at a medium temperature while stirring constantly.

Pour in the water, the cumin powder, the lemon juice (about 2 TBSP of it) and a pinch of salt. Bring this mix to a boil before adding the bulgur. After verifying that it is completely covered with water, bring it again to a boil, then take the pot off the heat and let the bulgur absorb the water for at least 45 minutes.

Meanwhile, rinse the spring onions and the tomatoes. Cut the onions into slices, core the tomatoes and dice them into bits as large as a finger. Peel the cucumber, then dice it into bits as large as a finger as well. After the 45 minutes have passed, mix the remaining oil with the bulgur and add the vegetables.

Variation: If you want to have a more intense flavor, add another TBSP of parsley and 1 TBSP of chopped mint leaves. The Kisir may also be served on a salad or some endive leaves.

The Kisir is in some ways the Turkish cousin of the Taboulé dish, while its main distinctive property is the fact that it is prepared with bulgur and not with semolina and it only rarely contains mint leaves.

Kuru Fasulye

Feeds 4

400 g of dried white beans
2 onions
2 cloves of garlic
400 g of peeled tomatoes
2 red chilies
2 TBSP of olive oil
2 vegetable stock cubes
1 TSP of salt
1 TSP of ground pepper
2 TSP of red paprika powder
1 TSP of chopped parsley
600 ml of water

The day before the preparation, it is recommended that you put the dry beans in a bowl with water so they can soak some of it up during the night. Should you have taken beans that were not dry, this step is not necessary. In any way, the beans will have to be washed in a sieve until the water pouring off is clear. Put them in a large pot afterwards, along with the water as well as the stock cubes, then bring the pot to the boil.

Rinse the chilies, core them, then cut them into thin rings. Peel the garlic and the onions, then chop them. Pour the oil into a small pot and heat it along with the onions and the garlic to medium temperature. Fry them for 1 to 2 minutes, then add the peeled tomatoes, the pepper, the paprika powder as well as the parsley.

Let this mixture simmer for 4 to 5 minutes, then pour it into the large pot with the beans. Dissolve the stock cubes in the water, then pour this in as well. Add the salt and let it simmer at medium temperature for 50 minutes. Stir regularly and in the end, taste and season if necessary.

The dish may also be accompanied by rice.

As with many other dishes from this region, the Kuru Fasulye has an intense taste and is one of the national dishes of Turkey, along with the Kebap and the Kofte (meatballs).

Lasagne

Feeds 4

500 g of Lasagne plates
800 g of peeled tomatoes
2 shallots
1 clove of garlic
*150 g of grated vegan cheese**
6 TBSP of neutral oil
1 vegetable stock cube
100 g of soy granulate*
50 g of wheat flour*
2 TBSP of olive oil
*500 ml of plant based milk**
*Powdered nutmeg**
1 TSP of salt
1 TSP of chopped oregano
1 TSP of chopped basil
250 ml of water

Preheat the oven at 200 °C. Prepare the tomato sauce by bringing the water along with the stock cube to a boil in a pot. Put the soy granulate into another pot and pour enough boiling vegetable stock over it, so that it covers the granulate entirely. Let it absorb the stock for 20 minutes.

Meanwhile chop the shallots as well as the garlic and fry them in a pan with the oil during 1 to 2 minutes at medium temperature. Add the soy granulate to the pan and let it simmer until all the water has evaporated. Put in the peeled tomatoes, the salt, the oregano, the basil as well as a pinch of pepper and bring it to a boil. Taste it and, if necessary, season with salt and/or pepper.

Prepare the white sauce in another pot by heating the oil in it, then pouring in the flour. Stir constantly for about 2 minutes at medium temperature, then add the milk and bring it to a boil for another 2 minutes, all while still stirring the entire time. Reduce the temperature to a medium level and add 2 TBSP of grated cheese as well as pinches of salt, pepper and nutmeg. Taste and season if necessary.

Grease a glass plate for the oven, cover its bottom with a fine layer of tomato sauce, then the first layer of Lasagna plates. Then comes another layer of tomato sauce, a fine layer of grated cheese. Repeat the process until you run out of plates or tomato sauce. Cover the last layer of plates with the white sauce and spread the remaining cheese over it. Put it into the preheated oven at 200 °C for half an hour.

At the time of the Roman Empire, a common earthenware bowl was designated as "lasanum" and throughout history, the Italians had begun using it to cook some of their pasta. Nowadays, a lot of Italian restaurants still serve their Lasagna "al forno", meaning "in the oven", in a similar bowl.

Lentil Stew

Feeds 6

Germany

500 g of potatoes
300 – 400 g of yellow lentils
3 carrots
2 TBSP of neutral oil (like sunflower)
6 TBSP of vinegar
1 TBSP of chopped parsley
1 TSP of chopped lovage (if available)
1 laurel leaf
3 cubes of vegetable stock
Salt and pepper
800 ml of water

First of all, if your lentils are dried, soak them in water for several hours, maybe even the night before preparing the stew. Anyway, before using them, rinse them in a sieve until the water pouring off is clear.

Peel the potatoes as well as the carrots, dice them into bits as large as a finger and chop the parsley if necessary.

Put the potato and carrot dices into a large pot along with the laurel leaf and pour the water in. Bring it to a boil and add the crumbled stock cubes, then reduce the temperature to a medium level and let it simmer for 20 minutes.

When these have passed, take out the laurel leaf and crush the contents partly with a potato masher. Add the lentils (without their water), as well as the parsley and the lovage. Put in a pinch of salt and pepper too, along with the vinegar and bring it to a boil for 1 minute while stirring, then reduce the temperature to a medium level.

Let it simmer for 20 more minutes while stirring regularly and then taste to check of the lentils are soft enough and if you need to season with salt, pepper and/or vinegar.

Variation: As the original recipe contains sausages that make up a part of its characteristic taste, you may add 5 to 6 vegan sausages (made of soy* for instance). Cut them into slices, heat up some oil in a pan and fry them at medium temperature until they have become golden in color. Add them just before serving.

The lentil stew represents one of the German cuisine's philosophies quite well: a satiating dish with local ingredients which will feed a whole family.

Mafé

Feeds 4

Senegal

300 g of kohlrabi
200 g of carrots
400 g of potatoes
1 onion
1 clove of garlic
2 TBSP of olive oil
1 vegetable stock cube
2 TBSP of soy sauce*
1 TBSP of curry powder
2 TSP of tomato puree
*5 TBSP of peanut butter**
Salt and pepper
Chili flakes
400 ml of water

Rinse and dice the vegetables into bits as large as a finger and finely chop the garlic and the peeled onion.

Heat the water along with the stock cube in a small pot while you heat the onion, the garlic and the curry powder with the oil in a large pot. Fry them for 1 to 2 minutes at medium temperature, then add the vegetable stock cube and the kohlrabi dices. Let them simmer for 5 minutes, then add the carrots and the potatoes. Put in the peanut butter, the tomato puree and the soy sauce, then stir this mixture.

Cover the pot and let it simmer at low temperature for half an hour while stirring regularly. In the end, taste it, and if necessary, season it with some more salt and pepper.

As for decoration, you may sprinkle some chili flakes on it.

Traditionally, the Mafé is a thick gravy-type sauce which is found in different variations throughout Africa where it is usually accompanied by rice or flat round bread and served with meat or fish.

Mapo Doufo

Feeds 4

China

2 cups of basmati rice
*400 g of plain tofu**
100 g of soy flakes*
6 cm of ginger
3 spring onions
3 TBSP of peanut oil
5 TBSP of soy sauce*
1 TBSP of spicy hot bean sauce ("Doubanjiang")
1 TSP of seasoned salt
1 clove of garlic
1 red chili
1 green chili (or another red)
1 TBSP of ground Sichuan pepper
450 ml of water
5 cups of water

Bring the water to a boil in a pot, then add the seasoned salt and the soy flakes. Let them simmer at medium temperature for 20 minutes, or until all the water has been absorbed while stirring regularly. Be careful to not let all the water evaporate too quickly and have the flakes stick to the bottom of the pot.

Dice the tofu into bits as large as a finger and cut the spring onions into rings. Place the tofu dices in a bowl and cover them in soy sauce to marinate them. Make sure all their sides are covered. Keep the green onion rings for decoration later on. Peel the ginger and grate it. Chop the garlic, core the chilies and slice them.

Put the rice into another pot and add the 5 cups of water to it. Bring it to a boil while stirring regularly until most of the water has been absorbed.

Now take a large pan or a wok, heat up the oil and fry the chilies, the garlic as well as the ginger during 1 to 2 minutes at medium temperature. Add the soy flakes including any remaining liquid and let it simmer until all the water has been absorbed.

In the end, add the tofu along with the soy sauce, the pepper, the white onion rings, the hot bean sauce as well as 10 ml of water and let it simmer for 5 to 8 minutes at medium temperature. Stir regularly, taste it and season as necessary.

The dish is served with rice; you may use the green onion rings and some oil droplets as decoration.

The Mapo Doufu has its origins in the Chinese central province of Sichuan which is well-known for its hot and spicy dishes. It is usually prepared with tofu, but depending on the region and season, other ingredients such as minced meat, may be put in as well. This dish is also known in other variations in Japan and Korea.

Minestrone

Italy

Feeds 4

2 carrots
*1 bundle of branch celery**
1 stem of leek
1 courgette
6 tomatoes
2 TBSP of tomato puree
100 g of mange-tout string beans
1 shallot
1 TBSP of chopped basil
1 TBSP of chopped parsley
300 g of small pasta (vermicelli)
2 TBSP of olive oil
2 vegetable stock cubes
1 TSP of salt
½ TSP of ground pepper
2 litres of water

Rinse all vegetables, then peel the carrots. Core the tomatoes, cut them into pieces as large as a finger and break the mange-tout into 2 or more pieces. Dice the carrots and the courgette into bits half as large as a finger. Take the leaves off the celery (maybe keep them as decoration for later), then cut the branches into half rings as large as half a finger.

Chop the shallot, the garlic as well as the basil and fry them in a large pot along with the oil at medium temperature for 1 to 2 minutes. Add the tomatoes for another 1 to 2 minutes and stir. Put in the remaining vegetables (except the mange-tout) as well as the tomato puree and let it simmer for 2 to 3 minutes.

In the mean time dissolve the vegetable stock cubes in the water, then pour it into the vegetable pot. Add the salt as well as the pepper, stir, cover the pot and let it simmer for 50 minutes at low temperature.

After this, put in the mange-tout and let it simmer for another 10 minutes at low temperature. Meanwhile, cook the pasta in another pot as indicated on its packaging, drain its water once it is done and put them it the soup pot. Taste and if necessary, season it with some salt and/or pepper.

Variation: Depending on the region in Italy, the contents of the Minestrone may vary a bit. Other ingredients are potatoes, green string beans, rice, slices of grilled bread, aubergine, mushrooms, pesto, lentils, or white cabbage.

The Minestrone is often served as a starter in Italian restaurants, while historically, it was a thick soup designed to be a complete meal. What is interesting though is that, even if it sometimes contains meat, it is rarely prepared with meat stock, but usually with vegetable stock.

Miso Soup

Japan

Feeds 4

*200 g of plain tofu**
2 carrots
2 spring onions
200 g of mushrooms (Shitake ideally)
1 pack of Wakame (Fucus)
2 TBSP of sesame oil*
1 vegan Miso stock cube
Salt and pepper
1 litre of water

Peel the carrots, cut them into thin bands as long as a finger. Rinse the spring onions, then cut them into slices as thick as half a finger and separate the white ones from the green ones. Clean the mushrooms and cut them into slices as large as half a finger. Dice the tofu into bits as large as half a finger and dissolve the Miso stock cube in the water.

Heat up the oil in a large pot, add the mushroom slices and fry them for 1 to 2 minutes at medium temperature while turning them often. Pour in the water with the Miso stock as well as the carrots, the Wakame cut into thin bands and the white spring onion rings. Bring the mix to a boil, then reduce the temperature to a medium level and let it simmer for 2 to 3 minutes. Add the tofu as well as pinches of salt and pepper. Reduce the temperature to a low level and let it simmer for another 2 to 3 minutes. Taste your soup and season if necessary.

Finally pour it into soup plates or bowls and use some of the green spring onion rings as decoration.

The Miso itself is a sort of paste (or stock cube), mostly made of fermented soy. You have to pay attention however as not to confuse it with the Dashi (which is based on fish), so it is important for vegetarians to verify the paste's contents.

Nems

Vietnam

Feeds 4

20 rice paper sheets
*200 g of plain tofu**
200 g of soy sprouts*
4 spring onions
1 small Chinese cabbage
1 carrot
1 clove of garlic
3 TBSP of soy sauce*
2 TBSP of sesame oil*
1 TSP of lemon juice
Salt and pepper
150 ml of water

Begin by dicing the tofu into bits as large as half a finger and marinate them in a bowl with the soy sauce and the lemon juice.

Cut the cabbage and the spring onions into thin slices. Peel then grate the carrot, chop the garlic and fry both of them in a large pan or wok along with the oil for 1 minute at a medium temperature. Add the cabbage, the onion slices and the tofu without its marinade (but keep it), let it heat up for a few moments, then pour the water in. Bring the pot to a boil and stir regularly until almost all the water has evaporated or has been absorbed. Reduce the temperature to a medium level, add the soy sprouts and the marinade, stir, taste and season if necessary with salt and/or pepper. Pour off any remaining water with the help of a sieve, then put the mix back into the pot.

Put one rice paper sheet onto a wet towel. Put 1 TBSP of the tofu-vegetable mixture in the middle of its lower half. Close down both sides on the mixture, then begin rolling the spring roll starting on the side with the mixture. It will take you a few tries but when it is done right, its "skin" will consist of 2 layers of rice paper.

The rolls may now be eaten "raw" like this or they can be fried in a large pan. To do so, pour enough sesame oil in your pan so that it forms a layer as thick as a finger and heat it up at a high temperature before adding them. Be careful that they do not touch each other, they will probably be very sticky. Turn them often until they have become crispy. Once this is the case, take them out and set them down on some kitchen paper to absorb the excess oil.

Note however that rice paper is a very delicate matter and quite sticky, you'll certainly need a few trials before they will be as they should.

As a well-known Asian delicacy, these rolls are to be found in all of South-East Asia. In China, they are served raw and called “spring rolls” at the occasion of the new Chinese New Year where they symbolize the silkworms that are hatching at the time. In Vietnam, they are fried and called “nems” and are usually served with a spicy fish sauce, while on the Philippines they are called “loempias”.

Onion Soup

Feeds 4

200 g of onions
80 ml of sunflower oil
1 TBSP of wheat flour*
*100 g of grated vegan cheese**
4 slices of bread
15 ml of Cognac (or red wine)
1 vegetable stock cube
Salt and pepper
1 litre of water

Chop the onions and heat the oil in a large pot. Put in the onions and let them simmer at a low temperature for 15 minutes while stirring regularly so they do not stick to the bottom. Meanwhile dissolve the stock cube in the water and preheat the oven at 200 °C.

Spread the flour on the onions, mix, then add the water with stock. Stir again, cover the pot and let is simmer for another 15 minutes at a medium temperature.

Cut the bread slices into small mouthfuls and roast them in a pan without any additional grease for 5 to 6 minutes while turning them often. When the soup is done, add the Cognac, taste it and season with salt and pepper.

Distribute the soup evenly between your plates, put a few pieces of roast bread on each and spread some grated cheese on top. Put them in the oven fir 2 to 3 minutes before serving. Careful though, the plates will be hot when you take them out of the oven.

Variations: **German Onion Soup:** For this variation, leave out the vegan cheese and instead of the Cognac, use the same quantity of red wine (preferably a German one). Traditionally, you'd put in some sour cream and a pinch of caraway and you can replace the sour cream by rice cream or vegetable milk.

The Onion soup is part of some European cuisines in some form or other, even though its origins are French and especially Parisian. It seems that it was already prepared during the 18th century and mostly eaten by merchants, their customers and poorer people.

Paella

Feeds 4

Spain

120 g of rice
1 red bell pepper
1 yellow bell pepper
2 tomatoes
200 g of small peas
200 g of artichoke hearts
1 shallot
1 clove of garlic
2 TBSP of olive oil
2 TBSP of red paprika powder
2 TSP of turmeric powder
1 vegetable stock cube
500 ml of water

Prepare the vegetable stock by bringing half of the water to a boil in one pot and dissolve the stock cube in it before reducing the temperature to a low level. Bring the other half of the water to a boil in another pot along with the rice, then reduce the temperature to a medium level and let it absorb the water for 20 minutes. Pay attention that it does not stick to the bottom of the pot. If there remains water after, pour it off. Meanwhile rinse and core the vegetables. Slice the bell peppers into thin bands as long as half a thumb, dice the tomatoes into bits as large as a finger and cut the artichoke hearts into quarters. Chop the garlic and the shallot.

Heat up the oil in a large pan along with the shallot and the garlic, fry them for 1 to 2 minutes at medium temperature, then add the bell peppers as well as the tomatoes and keep going for another 5 to 6 minutes while stirring regularly. Put in the rice, the turmeric, the paprika powder and the vegetable stock. Cover the pan and let it simmer for 20 minutes at low temperature.

Taste if the rice has softened enough before putting in the peas and the artichoke hearts. Cover the pan again and let it simmer for another minute before serving.

Variations: Instead of the turmeric, you may also use ½ TSP of saffron powder to give the paella its characteristic color. The rice may also be replaced by small pasta shaped like rice grains. You may also use green string beans which are cut into pieces as large as a finger and added along with the bell pepper.

The paella originates from the Spanish city of Valencia and it has to be noted that the word “paella” is not only used to describe the dish itself, but also for the large sort of pan in which the Spanish prepare it.

Palak Dal

Feeds 4

India

2 cups of rice
200 g of yellow lentils
200 g of spinach
1 TBSP of neutral oil (like sunflower)
1 TSP of mustard grains*
4 Bay leaves (or laurel leaves)
1 large shallot
4 cm of ginger
100 g of chopped tomatoes
2 red chilies
2 green chilies (or another 2 red ones)
2 cloves of garlic
1 TSP of cinnamon powder
1 TSP of cumin powder
200 ml of coconut milk
Salt and chili flakes
5 cups of water

At least 2 hours before beginning the preparation (preferably already the night before), it is recommended that you soak the lentils in water. Before preparation, bring a pot of water to a boil with the lentils in it and let it boil for 15 minutes until they are almost soft. In the meantime chop the garlic and the shallot, peel and grate the ginger, core the chilies and slice them into thin rings.

Heat up the mustard grains and the oil in a pan at high temperature until the grains start leaping. Reduce the temperature to a medium level and add the garlic, the shallot, the chilies, the ginger as well as the cumin and cinnamon powders. Fry this mixture for 1 minute while stirring constantly, then add the tomatoes and the bay leaves.

Put the spinach into the pan and let it heat up for a few moments, then add the lentils (after pouring off their water) and the coconut milk. Mix it well, then let it simmer at medium temperature for 5 to 8 more minutes.

In the meantime, prepare the rice by pouring it into another pot with the water and a pinch of salt. Bring it to a boil until most of the water has evaporated while stirring regularly to avoid the rice sticking to the bottom.

Finally, taste your dish and season it if necessary with some salt and/or chili flakes.

In Central Asia, yellow lentils are called “Dal” if they have been peeled. They may be part of a main course like in this recipe, but may also accompany other main courses as a side dish along with rice, then they are called “Dal Bhat”, which means “Lentils and rice”.

Peanut Stew

Feeds 4

Cameroon

1 small white cabbage
3 carrots
200 g of red beans
200 g of sweetcorn
200 g of tomato puree
1 red bell pepper
1 onion
*5 TBSP of peanut butter**
2 TBSP of neutral oil (like sunflower)
½ TSP of chopped thyme
1 TSP of red paprika powder
*1 TBSP of mustard**
2 TSP of ground pepper
1 TSP of salt
½ TSP of cumin
1 vegetable stock cube
3 TBSP of mango juice
300 ml of water

To begin with, rinse the white cabbage and cut it into mouthfuls. Peel the carrots and cut them into half-discs. Cook the both of them in a pot with boiling salted water for about 10 minutes, then pour the water off.

In the meantime, you can wash and core the bell pepper, then pour off the sweetcorn's and the beans' fluids. If the latter were dried, you should put them into a bowl of water the night before the preparation so they can absorb it. Peel the onion and dice it into pieces as large as a finger; do the same with the bell pepper. Dissolve the stock cube in the water. Take another large pot, pour in the oil and heat it at medium temperature. Add the onions and the bell pepper to fry them for 2 to 3 minutes. Put in the cumin, the mustard, as well as the pepper and roast them for a few moments before pouring in the tomato puree and the water with the stock.

Let it simmer for 4 to 5 minutes, then add the beans, the carrots, the cabbage, the sweetcorn, the thyme, the paprika powder, the salt and the peanut butter. Mix, then wait for it to heat up during 2 to 3 minutes while stirring regularly. Finally add the mango juice, stir again, taste and season some more with juice, salt and/or pepper.

The use of peanut butter is typical for the Central African cuisine, especially in stews or thick gravy-type sauces which normally accompany meat or rice dishes.

Penne all' Arrabbiata

Feeds 4

400 g of penne
300 g of tomato puree
3 red chilies
1 large shallot
1 clove of garlic
4 tomatoes
1 TSP of chopped basil
1 TSP of chopped parsley
1 TSP of ground pepper
½ TSP of salt
1 TBSP of balsamico vinegar
2 TBSP of olive oil

To begin with, rinse the tomatoes as well as the chilies and core them. Dice the tomatoes into bits as large as a finger or a bit less and slice the chilies into rings. Peel the shallot and the garlic, then chop them.

Heat up the oil in a small pot with the shallot and the garlic at medium temperature for 1 to 2 minutes, then add the tomato dices and the chili rings. Fry them for 1 minute while stirring constantly, then pour the tomato puree in, mix it, bring it to a boil for a few seconds, then reduce the temperature to a low level.

Add the vinegar, the basil, the parsley, the salt and the pepper. Stir, cover the pot and let the sauce simmer for 15 minutes at a low temperature.

Meanwhile bring some water to a boil in another large pot and cook the penne according to the instructions on their package.

You may serve the sauce on top of the penne, or you can mix them in the pot, so that the penne may absorb the sauce for 1 to 2 minutes before serving.

The arrabbiata sauce for accompanying pasta originates from Latium, the province in central Italy whose province capital is Rome itself. An interesting fact is that "arrabbiata" may be translated as "furious" or "passionate", which explains the quantity of chilies used as ingredients.

Pizza

Italy

Feeds 4

500 g of wheat flour*
1 red bell pepper
1 yellow bell pepper
200 g of mushrooms
200 g of artichoke hearts
200 g of black olive rings
400 g of tomato puree
*200 g of grated vegan cheese**
2 TBSP of olive oil
2 TSP of salt
1 TSP of sugar
1 portion of yeast (~40 g)
1 TSP of chopped basil
300 ml of water

To begin with, dissolve the yeast in the hand warm water and put the flour in a large bowl along with the salt. Pour in the water with the yeast, as well as the oil and the sugar. Mix, then knead it for a few minutes. You may do this with your hands, but the use of an electrical kitchen aid is recommended.

Once you are done kneading, put the dough into a bowl, cover it and let it rest for an hour in a warm place (like on a radiator). In the mean time you may prepare the vegetables and start the oven at 210 °C maybe half an hour later.

After rinsing all vegetables, cut the mushrooms into thin slices, pour off the liquid of the olives, cut the artichoke hearts into quarters, core then slice the bell pepper into thin bands. When the hour is up, you'll have enough dough for either 4 round pizzas or 2 oven trays. Divide your dough into 2 or 4 portions accordingly. Spread some flour on your work surface, then roll the dough out until it is as thin as half a finger or even less.

Once they are thin enough, spread a few TBSP of tomato puree on it, while taking care to get as close as half a finger's width to the border. Place the vegetables on it as you like, sprinkle the basil on top first and the vegan cheese after this.

Put the pizzas on a tray with baking parchment and insert them in the preheated oven at 210 °C for 10 to 15 minutes. Check regularly that the vegan cheese does not become too dark.

Variations: While there may be no need to mention it, other ingredients may decorate your pizzas as well like onion rings, pineapple rings or even spinach.

The "Margherita" pizza, with green basil leaves, white Mozzarella cheese and red tomatoes was apparently born when King Umberto Ist wanted his wife Margherita to taste a pizza from a local restaurant. The King was of course a patriot, so he had it prepared with the above-mentioned ingredients in the colors of the Italian flag.

Quesadilla

Feeds 6

12 wheat tortillas*
1 shallot
2 cloves of garlic
100 g of baked beans
*100 g of smoked tofu**
1 red bell pepper
2 red chilies
*300 g of grated vegan cheese**
2 TBSP of neutral oil (like sunflower)
Salt and pepper

Preheat the oven at 180 °C, then rinse the bell pepper as well as the chilies and core them. Chop the chilies, while you dice the tofu and the bell pepper into bits as large as half a finger. Pour the liquid off the beans, then place them on some paper towels to dry a little.

Chop the shallot and the garlic, then fry them in a pan along with the oil at medium temperature for 1 to 2 minutes. Add the tofu dices as well as a pinch of salt and pepper, then fry them until they have become lightly golden in color. Put them aside in a bowl.

Cover an oven tray with baking parchment and place 2 to 4 tortillas on it, depending on their size. On one half of each tortilla, first place a fine layer of grated cheese, then a thin layer of the tofu-vegetable mix and another thin layer of grated cheese. Be careful to put enough cheese close to the borders. Fold the other half on it and slightly press the edges. Do not worry if they are not 100% shut, normally the cheese will take care of this in the oven.

Put the tray into the preheated oven at 180 °C for 10 minutes while paying attention that the quesadillas do not become too dark in color.

Once they are out, cut them in half and serve them with salsa and/or guacamole sauce.

Variation: In Mexico, the typical ingredients for quesadillas include mushrooms and finely diced potatoes. They also include minced meat, which you can replace by 30 g of soy* flakes marinated for 20 minutes in soy* sauce before adding them (without the sauce).

One of the main differences between the quesadilla and similar dishes like fajitas or enchiladas is the fact that Mexican quesadillas are not rolled, but folded. They are of course also well-known in the Southern United States, but instead of folding, people here use two tortillas on top of each other, with the filling in between.

Ratatouille

France

Feeds 4

1 aubergine
1 red bell pepper
1 yellow bell pepper
1 courgette
400 g of peeled tomatoes
1 clove of garlic
1 shallot
5 TBSP of olive oil
1 TSP of chopped rosemary
1 TSP of chopped thyme
1 TBSP of sugar
1 TBSP of salt
50 ml of white wine
Salt and pepper
250 ml of water

Note that if you want to serve the Ratatouille alone without side dishes, you may want to prepare the double of the indicated quantities in order to satisfy 4 people.

Rinse the vegetables, then dice them into pieces as large as a finger, beginning with the aubergine. Put the aubergine dices in a sieve and cover them with the salt. That way, they can lose some of their water while you prepare the rest. Peel then chop the shallot and the garlic.

Pour 2 TBSP of oil in a large pot and heat it at medium temperature. Add the garlic as well as the shallot and let them fry for 1 to 2 minutes. Then put in the bell peppers and fry them for 2 to 3 minutes. Add the rosemary and the thyme, as well as the courgette dices, then fry them for another 3 to 4 minutes. Finally add the aubergine and let it simmer at medium temperature for 7 to 8 minutes while stirring regularly. Spread the sugar on top and keep going for another minute while stirring.

Pour in the wine, wait for 2 minutes while stirring a few times, then add the tomatoes and the water. Cover the pot and let it simmer for 20 minutes while stirring regularly. After this, remove the lid, add the remaining 3 TBSP of oil as well as a pinch of ground pepper and taste it. If necessary, season some more with salt and/or pepper.

The Ratatouille can be eaten on its own, but it can also be accompanied by boiled potatoes or rice.

After the worldwide success of the animated movie featuring the cooking rat, this name is known all over the globe. Fewer people however know that it has always been a vegan dish from its beginnings.

Ribollita

Italy

Feeds 4

300 g of white baked beans
2 shallots
6 slices of white bread
250 g of leaf celery
1 head of savoy cabbage
2 carrots
200 g of potatoes
400 g of peeled tomatoes
2 TBSP of olive oil
1 vegetable stock cube
½ TSP of chopped oregano
½ TSP of chopped thyme
½ TSP of chopped basil
Salt and pepper
1 litre of water

Ideally, this dish is prepared the night before serving it. If the beans are dried, they are preferably put in a bowl with water at least 12 hours before the preparation. When you begin to prepare them, boil them in a pot with enough water to cover them by a thumbs width at least and add a pinch of salt.

Then wash the beans in a sieve, put half of them away in a bowl for later and puree the other half with a hand blender. Peel the shallots, the carrots and the potatoes. Chop the shallots, then dice the carrots as well as the potatoes into pieces as large as half a finger. Dissolve the stock cube in the water. Wash the celery and the savoy cabbage, take off the celery's leaves, cut it into half-rings as large as half a finger and slice the savoy cabbage into thin bands.

Heat the oil in a large pot at medium temperature, then fry the shallots in it for 1 to 2 minutes. Add the carrots, the potatoes, the celery and the cabbage along with the tomato puree and the peeled tomatoes. Wait for a few moments to heat it up again, then slowly pour in the water with the vegetable stock. Let the pot simmer for 25 minutes or until the carrots have become soft enough. Add the beans (pureed and whole ones). Season with the oregano, the thyme, the basil as well as some salt and pepper, then taste the pot's contents.

Put half of the bread slices into another large pot and pour half of the soup over it, then add the second half of the bread slices and pour the remaining half of soup on top. You should now leave the soup alone for a few hours, so that the bread can soak up some of the fluid. Before serving, reheat the soup at medium temperature for about 10 minutes and stir until the bread slices have disintegrated.

A dish originating from the beautiful Tuscany region, it is known since the 19th century as “Tuscany farmer’s soup” and the name “Ribollita” was only used since the 1960’s.

Russian Skewers

Feeds 4

1 red bell pepper
1 yellow bell pepper
1 courgette
4 small onions
*400 g of smoked tofu**
6 TBSP of neutral oil (like sunflower)
350 g of tomato puree
1 vegetable stock cube
4 TBSP of soy sauce*
1 TSP of red paprika powder
Salt and pepper
200 ml of water

Preheat the oven at 100 °C.

Chop 1 onion and cut the tofu into pieces as thick as half a finger and as large as two thumbs. Dissolve the vegetable stock cube in the water.

Put the chopped onion into a pan or a pot, along with 2 TBSP of oil and let it fry for 1 to 2 minutes at medium temperature. Add the tomato puree and let them simmer for 1 minute at low temperature, then pour in the vegetable stock and bring the mixture to a boil, add pinches of salt and pepper, the paprika powder as well as the soy sauce. Stir, then taste and if necessary, season some more with salt and pepper. This sauce serves as a marinade too, so put the tofu in a bowl and pour the sauce over it. Turn the tofu pieces with a spoon to make sure each side is covered.

Rinse the courgette, cut it in two along its axis, then slice it as thick as half a finger. Cut the remaining 3 onions in a way to obtain pieces of roughly the same size. Wash the bell pepper, core them, then cut them to the same size as well.

Skew the tofu, the courgette, the bell pepper and the onions alternately on the skewers, then heat 4 TBSP of oil in a large pan at medium to high temperature and roast the skewers on each side for 4 to 5 minutes without letting them become too dark, then take them out and put them aside on a plate. You may even start reheating the sauce.

Finally, insert the skewers into the oven preheated at 100 °C for 5 to 7 minutes before serving. It has to be noted that while they can be roasted in a pan, they will taste better if they are grilled on a barbecue in summer and they are of course to be served with their sauce.

The Schaschlyk (with meat) is widely spread through Russia and Eastern Europe, but its origins lie in the Caucasian region. In Russia, it is usually accompanied by a cooked potato and a salad.

Sambhara

Feeds 4

2 cups of rice
1 large head of cauliflower
2 red chilies
1 yellow bell pepper
1 carrot
1 lemon
½ TSP of cumin powder
2 TSP of mustard grains*
3 TBSP of neutral oil (like sunflower)
Salt and pepper
5 cups of water

Rinse, clean and cut the cauliflower into small mouthfuls. Rinse and core the bell pepper and cut it into thin slices. Core the chilies as well and chop them. Press the lemon to obtain its juice, peel the carrot and cut it into thin bands long as half a thumb.

Boil the cauliflower in salted water for about 10 minutes, then pour the water off and set it aside.

Heat up the oil with the mustard grains in a large pan at high temperature until the grains start leaping. Add the cumin, stir, reduce the temperature to a medium level and fry for 1 to 2 minutes.

Meanwhile pour the rice, the water cups and a pinch of salt into a pot and heat them at high temperature until all the water has been absorbed.

Add the cauliflower, the bell pepper, the carrot and the chilies to the pan, then cook them for 4 to 5 minutes at a medium temperature. Taste if the cauliflower is soft enough and if necessary, season with salt, pepper and/or lemon juice (about 2 TBSP).

"Sambhara" can be translated from Sanskrit to "which reunites". As for this, it is not known if this relates to the different vegetables or to the family coming together for dinner.

Sauce: Salsa

Feeds 6

400 g of peeled tomatoes
1 red bell pepper
1 yellow bell pepper
2 shallots
2 red chilies
½ a lemon
2 TBSP of sugar
Salt and pepper

Rinse and core the bell peppers and the chilies, then dice the bell pepper into bits as large as half a finger or less and chop the chilies. Press the lemon to obtain its juice and chop the shallots.

Put the bell pepper dices, the chilies, the peeled tomatoes, 1 TBSP of lemon juice, the shallots, the sugar as well as a pinch of salt into a pot, mix it and let it simmer for 80 minutes at medium temperature while stirring regularly. Taste your sauce after and season it if necessary with pepper, salt, sugar and/or lemon juice.

This sauce is a classic that accompanies numerous Mexican and tex-mex dishes, but it also comes in handy for garden-parties and barbecues where it can be eaten with nachos.

Sauce: Mole Poblano

Feeds 8

100 g of red chilies (4 or 5)
1 vegetable stock cube
2 shallots
2 cloves of garlic
*80 g of peeled almonds**
*50 g of peeled peanuts**
1 TSP of ground pepper
½ of cinnamon powder
150 g of dark chocolate
6 TBSP of neutral oil (like sunflower)
100 g of tomato puree
500 ml of water

First heat 2 TBSP of oil in a pan and fry the chilies for 1 to 2 minutes at medium temperature, then put them in a pot with some water and let them simmer at low temperature for at least half an hour. Pour off the water, core them (or not, if you are more courageous), then puree them with a hand blender.

Meanwhile grate the chocolate, dissolve the stock cube in the 500 ml of water and chop the shallots as well as the garlic. Fry the both of them in a pan with 2 TBSP of oil for 1 to 2 minutes at medium temperature, then add the tomato puree and bring the mixture to a boil for a few seconds. Take the pot off the heat after.

Heat the remaining oil in another pan and put in the peanuts, the almonds, the pepper as well as the cinnamon and roast them for 2 to 3 minutes at high temperature. Mix the contents of both pans in a bowl and puree them with the hand blender.

Finally pour the chili puree and the contents of this bowl into a large pot and add the grated chocolate. Let it heat until the chocolate has melted, then pour in half of the vegetable stock. Let this mixture simmer at low temperature for 30 minutes while stirring regularly.

Taste your sauce, if it is too hot, add some sugar; if it is too thick, add some more vegetable stock.

The word "mole" refers to a large number of different sauces in the Mexican cuisine, most of which originate from the provinces of Puebla and Oaxaca. This mole sauce may also be served with enchiladas or other Mexican food.

Shirin Polo

Iran

Feeds 4

2 cup of Basmati rice
4 carrots
1 onion
2 TBSP of dried raisins
2 TBSP of dried barberries
*3 TBSP of chopped almonds**
1 TSP of cinnamon powder
4 cardamom capsules
2 TBSP of neutral oil (like sunflower)
Saffron powder
2 TSP of sugar
2 TSP of rose water (or orange juice)
Chopped parsley
Salt
5 cups of water

First of all, put the barberries into a bowl of water for half an hour. Peel the carrots and cut them into sticks as long as a thumb and as large as half a finger. Peel the onion as well and dice it into pieces as large as a finger.

Heat a large pot with the 5 cups of water and add a pinch of salt as well as the cardamom capsules, then the rice. Bring it to the boil until the rice has absorbed all the water. Stir regularly to prevent it from sticking to the bottom. Once the rice is done, takes the pot off the heat and remove the cardamom capsules.

Heat the oil in a large pan at medium temperature, then fry the onion dices and the chopped almonds in it for 1 to 2 minutes. Add the carrots and fry these for 2 to 3 minutes, then reduce the temperature to a low level. Put the barberries in, along with the dried raisins as well as the sugar and let it simmer for 4 to 5 minutes while stirring often.

Now pour the pan's content into the pot with rice, add the cinnamon powder, a pinch of saffron powder and the rose water. Mix, taste and season if necessary, then serve this dish on plates with a little chopped parsley as decoration.

Variations: Depending on the regions in Iran, you may also add ½ TSP of turmeric powder, chopped pistachios* and grated orange peels which was boiled for 5 minutes. Of course, you should wash your orange before grating it.

The origins of this name are not very clear. However, "Polo" designates a traditional rice dish in Iran; "Shirin" may be a reference to the queen Shirin, wife to the Persian king of kings at the beginning of the 7th century.

Soljanka

Feeds 4

Poland

3 onions
1 clove of garlic
*400 g of smoked tofu**
5 TBSP of neutral oil (like sunflower)
3 red chilies
400 g of tomato puree
10 small pickles
3 bay leaves
2 vegetable stock cubes
2 TBSP of plant based cream (or milk)
½ TSP of ground pepper
½ TSP of salt
Chopped parsley
Starch if necessary
1 litre of water

Rinse the chilies, core them and cut them into slices. Peel the onions and the garlic, dice the onions as large as a finger and chop the garlic. Cut the pickles into slices as large as half a finger and keep the liquid they were in. Dice the tofu into pieces as large as a finger.

Fry the tofu in a pan with some oil and salt at medium temperature for 5 to 6 minutes, then set it aside for later.

Heat the oil in a large pot at medium temperature and fry the onions, the tofu as well as the garlic for 2 to 3 minutes. Add the water and the stock cubes. Let it simmer for a few moments, then add the tomato puree, the bay leaves, the chilies, the pepper as well as the salt and mix it all.

Finally, add the pickle slices as well as the vegetable milk and let it simmer for 15 minutes in the covered pot, then add the tofu as well. Let the soup heat up again for 2 to 3 minutes, then remove the bay leaves, and serve it on plates while spreading some chopped parsley on top as for decoration. It should be a little thick, if this is not the case, add some starch.

Variation: You may replace the tofu by the same quantity of mushroom dices, which you fry in the pan with the onions and the garlic as well. You may also add some capers and/or olive rings.

Quite well known in Russia and Eastern Europe nowadays, this dish was also quite popular in the former German Democratic Republic. The Soljanka is mainly served with meat (replaced here by tofu), but is also found with mushrooms and with fish.

Spaghetti Bolognese

Italy

Feeds 4

100 g of soy granulate*
1 vegetable stock cube
2 TBSP of soy sauce*
1 large shallot
1 clove of garlic
300 g of peeled tomatoes
1 carrot
½ TSP of chopped basil
½ TSP of chopped thyme
2 TBSP of olive oil
500 g of spaghetti
Salt and pepper
600 ml of water

To begin with, bring 400 ml of water to a boil in a pot, then add 2 TBSP of the juice of the peeled tomatoes (without pulp), the stock cube, the soy sauce and the soy granulate. Mix, reduce the temperature to a low level and let the granulate absorb the fluid while you prepare the rest of the dish.

Peel the carrot and dice it into bits as large as half a finger. Chop the shallot as well as the garlic and fry them in a large pan along with the oil for 1 to 2 minutes at medium temperature. Add the soy mix, stir and let it simmer for 3 to 4 minutes at medium temperature. Pour in the peeled tomatoes, the carrot dices and the remaining 200 ml of water. Mix, then season with the basil, the thyme as well as pinches of salt and pepper.

Let the sauce simmer for another 20 minutes at medium temperature while you cook the spaghetti as indicated on their packaging.

Once the 20 minutes for the sauce are up, taste it and season if necessary.

The spaghetti bolognese are the classic of the Italian cuisine, and it is of course obvious that the sauce originates from the city of Bologna in Northern Italy. It is to be noted though that most locals however prefer tagliatelle instead of the spaghetti.

Sushi

Japan

Feeds 4

500 g of sushi rice
3 carrots
1 cucumber
10 Nori sheets (algae)
50 ml of rice vinegar
2 TBSP of Sake (or water)
1 TBSP of sugar
1 TSP of salt
2 TSP of Wasabi
Salt and pepper
Soy sauce*
Pickled ginger
*Sesame oil**
950 ml of water

Rinse the rice in a sieve until the water pouring off has become clear, then cook it in a covered pot at medium temperature for 10 minutes while paying attention that it does not stick to the bottom. When it is done, pour it into a large bowl to cool off. In a smaller bowl, mix the vinegar, 50 ml of water, the salt and the sugar, then add this to the rice and stir. Let it cool off now while you prepare the vegetables.

Peel the carrots as well as the cucumber and cut them into thin long sticks as large as half a finger or less. In a bowl, mix the Sake with the Wasabi; this will serve as "glue" later on for closing the rolls.

To roll a correct Maki-sushi, first lay a Nori sheet with its brilliant side facing down on a bamboo mat. Spread a portion of rice on three quarters of its surface. In the middle of the rice, trace a ditch where you place some of the ingredients of your choice. Begin rolling from the side opposite of the free quarter while leaving your fingertips on the ingredients so that they do not slip out. Once you reach the free quarter, gently pull the roll toward the side you started to tighten it, wet the free quarter with the Sake-Wasabi "glue", then finish rolling it completely. Repeat this process until you run out of rice, ingredients, or Nori sheets. Cut the rolls into pieces as large as a thumb with a very sharp knife. Should your knife tend to stick to the rolls after a few cuts, clean it, then continue.

The Maki-sushi are usually served with soy sauce, Wasabi and pickled ginger.

Variation: You may also use an avocado and/or mango cut into thin sticks.

The word "sushi" nowadays describes the multitude of different ways to prepare mainly raw fish and seafood with rice. The way described above is part of the "hoso-maki" subgroup, which translates to "fine roll".

Tagliatelle Aglio, Olio e Peperoncino

Feeds 4

400 g of tagliatelle
*100 g of grated vegan cheese**
3 cloves of garlic
5 red chilies
8 TBSP of olive oil
1 TSP of chopped parsley
½ TSP of chopped oregano
½ TSP of ground pepper
Salt

Cook the tagliatelle in a large pot of boiling salted water, according to the instructions on their packaging. When they are "al dente", pour the water off and keep them warm.

In the meantime prepare the sauce by cutting the garlic cloves into very thin slices with a sharp knife. Rinse the chilies and core them (or not if you are brave enough) and chop them finely.

Pour the oil into a pan and fry the garlic, the parsley, the oregano, the pepper as well as the chilies in it for 1 to 2 minutes at medium temperature while paying attention that the garlic does not become brown in color. If it should somehow be the case, immediately take the pan off the heat.

When the tagliatelle are ready, pour the water off, put them back into their pot, add the sauce from the pan, mix and serve your dish with some grated vegan cheese on top.

According to legend, the opulent hairstyle of the Italian princess Lucrezia Borgia at her marriage with Alfonso 1st had inspired a local chef to create pasta that resembled it, thus giving birth to the tagliatelle.

Tapas: Patatas Bravas

Feeds 4

2 shallots
1 clove of garlic
400 g of peeled tomatoes
3 chilli peppers
400 g of potatoes
2 TBSP of white wine
4 TBSP of olive oil
1 lemon
½ TSP of ground pepper
½ TSP of salt
Salt and pepper

To begin with, peel the potatoes and dice them into bits as large as a finger. Rinse, core (or not) the chilies and cut them into thin rings. Chop the garlic as well as the shallots and press the lemon to obtain its juice.

Fry the shallots and the garlic in a pan along with 2 TBSP of oil for 1 to 2 minutes at medium temperature. Add the peeled tomatoes, the chilies, the lemon juice and the white wine, mix and let it simmer for 20 minutes at medium temperature while stirring regularly.

Meanwhile, fry the potatoes in another large pan with 2 TBSP of oil at medium temperature until they have obtained a golden color, which should take about 10 minutes. Reduce the temperature to a low level and let them simmer for 15 more minutes before adding the sauce. Taste to check the sauce and if the potato dices are soft enough. If necessary, season with salt and/or pepper.

Let the potato dices absorb the sauce for 1 to 2 more minutes, then serve them.

Please note that tapas are always served as multiple dishes, so one alone does not constitute an entire meal for four people.

“Patatas bravas” may be translated to “potatoes for the brave”, which is not surprising, considering the amount of chilies in their sauce.

Tapas: Sherry Mushrooms

Spain

Feeds 4

500 g of small white mushrooms
2 shallots
3 cloves of garlic
2 red chilies
2 TBSP of chopped parsley
100 ml of Sherry (or white wine)
2 TBSP of olive oil
Salt and pepper

Rinse the mushrooms, cut them into quarters and chop the shallots as well as the garlic. Wash the chilies, core them (or not if you are brave enough) and cut them into thin rings.

Heat the oil in a large pan and fry the shallots, the garlic and the chilies during 1 to 2 minutes at medium temperature. Add the mushrooms, stir and let them simmer for 5 minutes while turning them regularly. Then pour in the sherry (or white wine) and let it simmer for 1 more minute.

Pour off the sherry with the help of a sieve, put the mushrooms back into the pan, spread the parsley over them and add pinches of salt and pepper. Taste it and if necessary, season with some more salt and/or pepper.

The tapas are an integral part of the Spanish cuisine; they are small dishes which are served along with empty plates for the guests and each of them helps himself/herself to the things he or she wants. To offer your guests a Spanish tapas evening, you will need to prepare a few of these small dishes.

The sherry is a Spanish white wine which has the same body and soul as the Spanish red wines, which are known to be dry and strong.

Thai Curry with Tofu

Feeds 4

Thailand

2 cups of basmati rice
*400 g of smoked tofu**
5 TBSP of soy sauce*
1 TSP of ground pepper
4 spring onions
200 g of carrots
2 TBSP of neutral oil (like sunflower)
60 g of red curry paste
Salt
1 TSP of sugar
400 ml of coconut milk
*Unsalted peanuts**
1 TBSP of corn starch
5 cups of water

To begin with, dice the tofu into bits as large as a finger. Pour the soy sauce into a bowl and mix it with the ground pepper, put in the tofu and make sure all of its surfaces are covered in oil.

Peel the carrots, cut them into thin slices, rinse the spring onions and slice them as well, but as large as half a finger. Put the green slices aside and the white ones into a wok (or a large pan) along with the oil and fry them for 1 to 2 minutes at medium temperature. Add the carrots which you fry for another 1 to 2 minutes before putting in the tofu (without the soy sauce) which you will leave in the pan for yet another 2 to 3 minutes.

Pour in the curry paste, the coconut milk, the soy sauce, the corn starch and a pinch of salt, stir it and let it simmer for 10 minutes at medium temperature. In the meantime, crush the peanuts and cook the rice by putting it into another pot with the water as well as a pinch of salt and boiling it until all the water has been absorbed.

When the curry mixture is ready, taste it and if necessary, season it with sugar or salt. The dish is then served with rice and as for decoration, green spring onion slices and crushed peanuts on top.

This dish is derived from the "Kaeng Phet" ("Hot soup") and adapted as a hot sauce for tofu and rice. Traditionally, each household in Thailand has a mortar for crushing the ingredients of their local red curry paste.

Thai Satay Noodles

Feeds 4

150 g of broccoli
1 red bell pepper
50 g of mange-tout
300 g of spaghetti noodles
*3 TBSP of peanut butter**
3 TBSP of sweet Thai chili sauce
100 ml of coconut milk
1 vegetable stock cube
3 TBSP of soy sauce*
4 TBSP sesame oil*
4 cm of ginger
100 g of baby corn
1 clove of garlic
1 shallot
*25 g of unsalted peanuts**
100 ml of water

First rinse the broccoli, the bell pepper and the mange-tout, then cut the broccoli into small mouthfuls and cook it for 10 minutes in boiling salted water. Core the bell pepper and slice it into fine bands as long as half a thumb, while you cut the mange-tout and the baby corn into three or four pieces each.

Peel and grate the ginger, chop the garlic and the shallot. Dissolve the stock cube in a bowl with the water, add the sweet Thai chili sauce, the peanut butter, the coconut milk as well as the soy sauce and stir.

Cook the noodles according to the instructions on their package, but with 2 TBSP of oil additionally. Pour off the excess water when they are done and put them aside in a bowl. Heat up 2 TBSP of oil in a wok or large pan and fry the garlic, the shallot as well as the ginger for 1 to 2 minutes at medium temperature. Add the baby corn, the bell pepper as well as the broccoli and let it simmer for another 2 to 3 minutes.

Pour in the prepared sauce, then add the mange-tout and bring it to a boil for a few seconds. Reduce the temperature to a medium level, add the noodles and let it simmer for 1 to 2 minutes before tasting it. Season if necessary, then put the dish on plates with some peanuts on top as decoration.

When it comes to table customs, one might imagine that Thailand would be like most of South-East Asia and almost everybody would eat with chopsticks. This was the case until the 19th century, when King Mongut decided to use fork and spoon, as he hosted a lot of European dignitaries. This custom was then rapidly adopted by the rest of the population.

Thiebou-dienne

Senegal

Feeds 6

2 cups of plain rice
*200 g of plain tofu**
3 potatoes
2 aubergines
4 carrots
3 shallots
200 g of tomato puree
4 TBSP of neutral oil (sunflower)
1 clove of garlic
3 red chilies
1 TBSP of chopped parsley
5 TBSP of soy sauce*
½ TSP of salt
½ TSP of pepper
Salt and pepper
6 cups of water

Dice the tofu into bits as large as a finger, put it into a bowl with the soy sauce, stir carefully and let it marinate while you prepare the rest of the dish. Peel the potatoes as well as the carrots and dice them into pieces as large as a finger as well. Chop the shallots and the garlic, then rinse, core and thinly slice the chilies. Wash the aubergines, cut off their ends and dice them into bits as large as a finger.

Heat up the oil in a large pot and fry the garlic, the shallots and half of the chilies in it for 1 to 2 minutes at medium temperature. Pour in the tomatoes as well as the rest of the chilies, stir and let them simmer for 2 minutes at medium temperature.

Put in the remaining vegetables, 1 cup of water as well as pinches of salt and pepper. Mix, then let them simmer for 25 minutes at medium temperature while stirring regularly. Add the parsley and the tofu (without the soy sauce) and keep going for 5 more minutes. Taste and season if necessary.

Meanwhile, pour the rice and 5 cups of water with a pinch of salt in a pot and boil it until all the water has been absorbed.

The name of this dish originates in a language spoken in Western Africa and roughly translates to “Fish with rice”. The fish in question is filled with a spicy onion mix and cooked until it is mixed with the sauce and the rice.

Tofu Vindaloo

Feeds 4

India

400 g of plain tofu
400 g of peeled tomatoes
2 cups of basmati rice
5 (or more) dried red chilies
½ TSP of cumin powder
1 TSP of coriander
1 TSP of black pepper grains
1 TSP of mustard grains
1 TBSP of turmeric powder
1 TBSP of vinegar
2 onions
1 clove of garlic
3 cm of ginger
400 ml of coconut milk
½ TSP of cardamom powder
4 cardamom capsules
½ TSP of cinnamon powder
1 TBSP of sugar
2 TBSP of neutral oil (like sunflower)
½ TSP of salt
5 cups of water

To begin with, please note that this sauce may be very hot and spicy and to take out a bit of its kick, you should use less chilies. Put the cumin, the coriander, the mustard and the pepper grains as well as the chilies (without their green ends) in a pan and roast them for 2 to 3 minutes at high temperature. Put them in a mortar and grind them to a puree. Pour it into a bowl, add the sugar, the vinegar and the salt, mix and put the bowl aside.

Peel the onions, the garlic and the ginger, chop the first two while you grate the latter. Heat the oil in a large pan, put in the onions, the garlic, the ginger as well as the turmeric and fry them for 2 to 3 minutes at a medium temperature. Pour in the coconut milk, the peeled tomatoes, the cardamom powder as well as the cinnamon and let it simmer until the tomatoes have mostly disintegrated. Add the chili puree, mix and let it simmer while you dice the tofu as large as a finger. Put these dices into a pan with some oil and fry them for 8 to 10 minutes. Add them to the sauce and let it simmer for another 10 minutes at a lower temperature. Taste and season if necessary.

Pour the rice, the cups of water, the cardamom capsules and a pinch of salt into a pot and cook the rice at high temperature until it has absorbed all the water. Stir regularly to prevent it from sticking to the bottom. Once it is done, take out the cardamom capsules and serve it along with the tofu in its sauce.

According to legend, the Vindaloo sauce was created in the past centuries in the city of Goa, which was the capital of the Portuguese colonies in India. It was served with meat on exceptional occasions. Nowadays, this dish has found its way into the Indian restaurants and can be enjoyed on every day, be it exceptional or not.

Yosenabe

Feeds 4

Japan

250 g of Asian Vermicelli noodles
10 Shitake mushrooms
*200 g of plain tofu**
4 carrots
1 Chinese cabbage
2 spring onions
3 TBSP of rice wine (or white wine)
4 TBSP of soy sauce*
2 TSP of lemon juice
½ TSP of ground pepper
1 vegan Miso stock cube or 1 TBSP of Miso paste (or a vegetable cube)
1 TSP of salt
1 litre of water

Cut the noodles as long as a finger, then cook them as indicated on their package, pour off the water afterwards. Rinse the mushrooms and slice them, while you dice the tofu into pieces as large as a finger. Wash the Chinese cabbage and cut it into bands as large as a finger. Peel the carrots and cut them into thin oblique slices. Rinse the spring onions and cut it into thin rings, separate the white ones from the greens ones after this.

Pour the water in a large pot, bring it to the boil and dissolve the stock cube in it. Add the carrots slices as well as the cabbage bands and let it boil for 4 to 5 minutes. Then pour in the mushrooms, the white spring onions rings, the tofu, the salt as well as the soy sauce and let it simmer at medium temperature for 4 to 5 minutes. Season with the wine, the lemon juice as well as the pepper and taste it. Season some more if necessary. Finally add the Vermicelli and let them heat up briefly.

To serve it, pour the soup into bowls and spread some green spring onion rings on it.

“Yose” roughly translates to “put together”, which indicates that (almost) all ingredients of this dish are cooked together in one pot and also that in Japan, all guests eat out of the same pot. A variation of this dish (with a lot more meat) is very popular with Sumo ringers, as its repeated consumption aids them in gaining the necessary weight.

End note

To conclude this book, please note that most of these recipes are derived from dishes containing meat and even with ingredients like smoked tofu, it is difficult to obtain the "original" flavor of meat. While the vegetarians will certainly approve of this, some others around the table may will not. It was not the intention of this book to deliver recipes for meatless dishes that taste exactly the same, but rather offer new alternatives and variations.

Please note that the author declines all responsibility for allergies or food intolerances, whether they are known or not, that may result from ingredients used in this book's recipes. Also, the author declines all responsibility for injuries occurred due to improper use of kitchen tools and accessories.

Find us on social media!

Year of first publication: 2020

Printed in Poland
by Amazon Fulfillment
Poland Sp. z o.o., Wrocław

73803245R00074